the fulcrum within reach of our grasp as liberators who recast CTSD (Continuing Trauma Stress Disorder) into a revolutionary catalyst."

Joy James, *PhD, Williams College; Author of* New Bones Abolition: Captive Maternal Agency and the (After)Life of Erica Garner

"Outland and Noel's Justified is a passionately-argued exploration of one of the most important domestic catastrophes of our day. Offering voices too rarely centered in public debate, the book seeks and stays with the families and communities of children and teens killed by police. A vital project."

Micol Seigel, *PhD, Indiana University; Author of* Violence Works: State Power and the Limits of Police and Uneven Encounters: Making Race and Nation in Brazil and the United States

THE IMPACT OF POLICE KILLINGS ON THE FAMILY AND COMMUNITY OF YOUTH VICTIMS

This work highlights survivors' voices in the exploration of police violence and homicide in the United States. Making vital connections between U.S. colonialism, structured and deputized violence, history of policing, and armed resistance by grassroots movements, the authors expand readers' understanding of the purpose of U.S. policing.

Responding to data that showed that in 2016 and 2017, more than 135 children and teens lost their lives to police violence, the author team traveled to multiple locations across the United States to sit with, learn from, and capture survivors' stories and experiences. Utilizing in-depth and public interviews, the book presents breathtaking, honest, and heart-wrenching narratives surrounding the impact of youth killed by police on the family, community, and activists. This book makes important connections between colonialism, the history of police corruption, and police killings of marginalized groups. Survivors' narratives provide important, nuanced information surrounding the impact of youth killed by police, often with impunity, on friends, family, and loved ones of the victims.

Synthesizing these stories with an overview of the state of policing in the United States, this scholarship extends recommendations and strategies for organizers, activists, students, and scholars to redefine public safety, as well as police power and accountability, in Black, Brown, Indigenous, and poor communities.

Rafael Outland, PhD, is an assistant professor in the Department of Counseling and School Psychology at Alfred University in Alfred, NY.

Thomas Noel, Jr., PhD, is an assistant professor in the Department of Advanced Studies, Leadership, and Policy at Morgan State University in Baltimore, MD.

THE IMPACT OF POLICE KILLINGS ON THE FAMILY AND COMMUNITY OF YOUTH VICTIMS

Justified

Rafael Outland and Thomas Noel, Jr.

Routledge
Taylor & Francis Group
NEW YORK AND LONDON

Designed cover image: Routledge

First published 2026
by Routledge
605 Third Avenue, New York, NY 10158

and by Routledge
4 Park Square, Milton Park, Abingdon, Oxon, OX14 4RN

Routledge is an imprint of the Taylor & Francis Group, an informa business

ISBN: 978-1-041-12658-4 (hbk)
ISBN: 978-1-041-12657-7 (pbk)
ISBN: 978-1-003-66591-5 (ebk)

DOI: 10.4324/9781003665915

Typeset in Galliard
by Apex CoVantage, LLC

R.O.: I dedicate this work to my daughters, Kaya and Talia. Thank you both for inspiring me. I further dedicate this work to youth victims killed by police in the United States. Your stories must be heard and memories uplifted.

T.N.: I dedicate this work to the victims, survivors, and loved ones who have and continue to experience state and deputized violence and police terrorism. Thank you for trusting us and allowing us to share your stories and counterstories. You live on and elevate this work.

Rest In Power!

CONTENTS

FIGURES

ABOUT THE AUTHORS

Rafael Outland, native of College Park, GA, is a father, counselor educator, youth advocate, organizer, and critical researcher and scholar. He has worked as a professor in academia for eight years. His critical research and scholarship are grounded in understanding and giving voice to the lived experiences of marginalized youth, their families, and their community. Dr. Outland, along with Dr. Noel, is a co-founder of *Critical Research Group (CRG)*, a space for researchers and scholars to build, analyze, and discuss components of critical research in a safe and supportive environment.

Thomas Noel, Jr. is from Irvington, NJ and is a researcher, scholar, and educator who has held positions in the areas of teaching, administration, and instructing roles in early childhood–12 and higher education settings. His research is grounded in critical humanism with humanity and dignity for all. He is the co-founder of *Critical Research Group* (CRG), a brave space for researchers and scholars to build community and discuss critical research. Noel's research focuses on collaborations between higher education institutions and high schools and community organizations for socially responsible leadership development and civic and community engagement with youth. His collaborative research with Dr. Rafael Outland addresses how families and communities are impacted when youth lose their lives to state violence.

ACKNOWLEDGMENT

To begin this acknowledgment, we want to give thanks to the Creator and the Ancestors for giving us strength, courage, and guidance to produce the book.

Next, there are several individuals we want to acknowledge for all the support, encouragement, and trust involved in producing this work. First, we want to extend sincere gratitude to the research team. These individuals included Kristofer Rounsville (M.S., mental health counselor), Asia Abraham (M.S., school counselor), Dr. Tomas Boatwright, and Dr. Craig Wahleed. Thank you for your time, commitment, compassion, and support during fieldwork, data analysis, and beyond. Many thanks to Kris and Tomas for the many moments to *Ground*, learn together, and support each other during our travels.

In addition, we want to thank the families, especially mothers and siblings, as well as community members of youth killed by police. We cannot say enough about our gratitude for welcoming us into your community, school, and at times, homes. Moreover, our deepest gratitude for trusting and believing in us to accurately relay your stories to the public. Finally, thank you to the auntie of one youth survivor in L.A. who fed and cared for us after the interview. We will never forget this sincere act of Love and Care, as you noticed we were "hot, thirsty, and hungry!"

Furthermore, we want to thank our editorial team, Ellen Boyne and Kate Taylor, editors from Routledge books and Taylor & Francis publishing, respectively. To Ellen, thank you for believing in the importance of this work reaching the public from the beginning. We further extend our gratitude to you and Kate for trusting our ideas and vision for the book cover design, layout, and structure. Overall, we are grateful for your partnership throughout the process to produce this book.

Finally, we want to thank all of our family and community members for the unwavering support during this project. Our deepest gratitude for the encouragement and push for us to "keep going" with the work and providing a safe space for us to vent and discourse about our experiences. Indeed, an active listening ear and a compassionate heart can be priceless! Moreover, many thanks to the Noel family for feeding and sheltering us during our travels in New Jersey and Illinois.

In conclusion, since this work is about youth killed by police, we want to extend our gratitude to all deceased youth victims from our project and beyond. May we all continue to respect and uplift your lives, legacies, and memories, while forwarding the struggle to hold police accountable for your untimely demise. Rest In Power!

1

A CAUTION TO THE READER

Our Journey That Led to This Work

The purpose of this book is to raise awareness of police terrorism and violence in Black and Brown communities, more specifically Black and Brown youth. Therefore, the intended audience of this book are those who are interested in learning more about the impact of this epidemic and who seek to organize change toward the abolition of policing as it currently exists in the United States. During 2016–2017, at least 135 children and adolescents between the ages of 9 months and 19 years were killed by police in the United States (Outland et al., 2020). Given these stunning statistics, we constructed this book to inform interested readers, activists, freedom fighters, organizers, educators, counselors, parents, families, and the general public of these atrocities for which more than 95% of these cases were *Justified* (Outland, 2021). Moreover, we acknowledge that there may be some readers who are staunch and loyal advocates of police and policing and who sternly oppose any work, such as this book, that reveals the impact of policing and police killings of children and adolescents on their loved ones. Thus, we also share this work with these individuals with the hope that they will openly read and listen to the powerful stories, narratives, and counter-narratives offered by the families, loved ones, friends, and communities of these children and adolescents.

In his book, *The End of Policing*, Vitale (2018) argues that the police and policing have strong supporters who seek to strengthen policing and *law and order* in the United States through continued surveillance, tracking, and the occupation of the Black, Brown, and Indigenous proletariat, and impoverished communities. Thus, we argue that calls for police abolition and to defund the police have shown limited to no improvement or transformation

DOI: 10.4324/9781003665915-1

FIGURE 1.1 WARNING/Safe School Zone sign near a local park in Chicago, IL.

to the phenomenon of citizens killed by police in the United States, along with police militarization. These calls, "the so-called police reforms," and actions by activists and lawmakers have yet to put a dent in the 1000s of citizens each year who were killed by police with impunity, over the past decade (Mapping Police Violence, 2022). As a result, in order to transform the phenomenon of police terror of U.S. citizenry, primarily youth, then it is necessary to understand the historical purpose of policing (what it is), its connection to colonialism, capitalism, and the State (function served), and its impact on survivors of police terror (Kraska, 2007; Mowatt, 2022; Seigel, 2018). We invite you, the reader, to read our work and reflect on the impact of police killings of youth in the United States. We ask that you remain open-minded and seek to engage in dialogue, conversation, discourse, and reflection with others – what the late bell hooks described as *radical openness*. Hooks (2003) introduced and believed that the most positive outcome of open dialogue was a commitment to *radical openness*. She suggests that *radical openness* is "the will to explore different perspectives and change one's mind as new information is presented" (Hooks, 2003, p. 48). Toward this end, we ask that you join us and others on this journey.

Caution to Readers

As you continue reading, please caution against trivializing the deaths of children and teens by police. Trivializing in the sense that these youth who were killed by police are more than *mere numbers to be equated and dissected*. Yet, they are the lives of children who were sons, daughters, classmates, teammates, friends, cousins, nieces and nephews, as well as intimate partners of others who loved them dearly. Thus, the necessity to frame survivors' narratives from this work within a historical context of colonial and state-sanctioned trauma, violence, and exploitation of oppressed bodies is of high importance (Fanon, 2004; Hill, 2010; Mowatt, 2022; Seigal, 2018; Scheper-Hughes & Bourgois, 2004)! This perspective is paramount in order for readers to truly observe, acknowledge, and embrace the continued suffering and hardships of survivors of youth killed by police, along with answers to "why" the State condones these acts, or simply *Justifies* them.

Police Killings of Youth: Phases I and II

In order to understand the importance of this work and why we researchers are summoned to pursue it, readers must first understand the origin of our research trajectory. This work originally began in 2012 following the killing of Trayvon Martin by self-appointed vigilante, George Zimmerman (Coates, 2013). At the time, Dr. Noel and Dr. Outland were both doctoral students at the University of Rochester, Warner School of Education. Dr. Outland's focus was on Counseling and Counselor Education, while Dr. Noel's trajectory surrounded Education Policy. We vividly recall learning the news of Trayvon's tragic murder from several news outlets, followed by the city of Rochester, NY citizenry responding in public uproar and protest. As an invited speaker at a local protest, I asked myself and attendees at the moment, "What Can We Do to Protect Our Children From State-Sanctioned Violence?" We needed to do something, and as training doctoral students, we felt it was our duty to partake in local organizing, protest, and speak out efforts (Rodney, 1969/1996).

Phase I: Children and Teens Killed by Police

On August 4, 2014, Michael Brown was killed by Ferguson, Missouri police officer, Darren Wilson (Hill, 2017). This killing of an unarmed teen by police, followed by Ferguson Uprising and Resistance in the days and months that followed (Kaba, 2021, pp. 54–55), was the original spark that moved us to pursue this project. Specifically, as doctoral students, Dr. Outland and Dr. Noel began a journey of capturing public narratives surrounding police terrorism and killings of youth. Armed with a video camera, microphone, interview protocol, and notepad, we traveled to different areas of Rochester, NY that drew public traffic, including but not limited to shopping plazas, grocery stores, neighborhoods, as well as youth and community organizations. We completed 6 in-depth interviews with local youth advocates and leaders and 15 public interviews with local residents. We further partook in listening and analysis sessions, which gave us time, space, and opportunity to make meaning of the collective stories. Although this early research as doctoral students was not published in a peer-reviewed journal, nor did we facilitate public presentations on the material, the experience provided us insights on *how* to conduct critical research of this caliber. Critical Research can be understood as scientific inquiry and analysis designed to 1) speak truth to power and 2) give voice to the unheard populus, or the oppressed (CRG323.org, 2024).

This experience led to Dr. Outland's original pursuit and discovery of the website formerly known as "KilledByPolice.net" in spring 2017. From its origin, this website chronicled police killings of "all" citizens (youth and adults) from 2013 and beyond. The database was the first of its kind, which included the name, date, location, web link for reference, as well as an image of the deceased. Readers should be informed that this website and information did exist, despite current evidence during a Google search that provides a website for "gun reviews and buying guides." Thus, readers are encouraged to visit the website, *Mapping Police Violence* (Mapping Police Violence, 2022), for statistical evidence on police killings in the United States.

After reviewing the database in 2016 and most of 2017, Dr. Outland noticed a major phenomenon that had been given limited to no recognition by scholars and researchers: Killings of children and teens by police. Indeed, awareness of some youth losing their lives to public violence was known by most. Yet, the frequency of youth killed by police was rarely discussed in mainstream news and/or media outlets. Some would argue that this fact still rings true to this day (Current Date: May 2025). Thus, Dr. Outland compiled an original archive of children and teens killed by police from the database titled "KilledbyPolice.net." Basic quantitative statistics were conducted on the data, which provided baseline information of frequency and categorical identifiers (age, gender, and race) of children/teens killed by police.

In the end, we discovered that from 2016 to August 31, 2017, 116 children and teens were killed by law enforcement. Specifically, 63 youth were killed in 2016 and 53 in 2017 (Outland, 2021, p. 228). Thus, *youth in general were killed by police every 72–120 hours (average three to four days)*. The youngest victim was 9 months old and the oldest 19, and the average age of most victims was 17 years old. Males were killed at an exponentially greater rate (N = 108) than females (N = 8), and Black males (N, MFB = 53) were twice as likely to be killed by police than their White (N, MFW = 24) and Latino counterparts (N, MFL = 23). The most disturbing phenomenon of the discovery was that all law enforcement officers were found by the courts *Justified* for their actions in taking the lives of youth victims (Outland, 2021, p. 229).

As a result of this conclusion, it became necessary and relevant to capture the narratives, lived experiences, and histories of the survivors of youth victims of police killings (i.e., mothers, fathers, siblings, friends, neighbors, teachers, etc.). Due to the reality that death by traumatic event (i.e., police killings and homicide) carries the potential to cause short- and long-term adverse effects on individuals, psycho-social (Kristensen et al., 2012), emotional (Nakajima et al., 2012; Smith, 2015), and physical functioning (Obasogie & Newman, 2017), it was apparent that the loved ones of youth victims of police killings were impacted by these youth's untimely deaths. Thus, Dr. Noel and Dr. Outland continued collecting the names and identifiers of youth victims killed from September to December 2017. In total, at least 135 children and teens were killed by police in 2016 and 2017 (Outland et al., 2020). These details, discoveries, and ambition to capture the stories of survivors fueled our determination to move to the second phase of this project.

Phase II: Impact of Police Killings on the Family and Community of Youth Victims

This phase of the project was exploratory in nature (Charmaz, 2014), in which the team sought to understand the lived experiences of the family and loved ones of youth killed by police (Outland et al., 2020). Children and teens killed by police archival data (Outland, 2021) was used as the database for identifying youth victims. This research took place over two years (2018 and 2019) and the team traveled to five states (East Coast, West Coast, and Midwest United States) and multiple cities to capture the narratives of survivors of youth killed by police.

During the first year, the team traveled to New York, New Jersey, and Maryland. Thirty-five adults supported the work, in which the team completed 25 public interviews and 10 in-depth ones (Outland et al., 2020). We were fortunate to capture several in-depth interviews with youth victims' loved ones, including a mother and aunt, a cousin and two news reporters, as well as three clergy. Snowball sampling was a useful approach to further identify individuals willing to share experiences regarding the impact of youth killed by police on their daily lives. Major themes derived from individuals' stories included *Living with Trauma, Meaning of State Violence, and Experiences of Police Intimidation* (Outland et al., 2020). Moreover, *Coming Together and Holding Police Accountable* evolved as major themes to end police killings of youth. Specifically, coming together involves a time to heal for survivors and community members as well as to develop strategies to protect youth from police terrorism. Furthermore, strategies must extend from the wounded minds and hearts of those left to relive and endure the absence of their deceased friend, cousin, or neighbor. In other words, solutions and strategies that may be useful to end police killings should not derive from outsiders, but from individuals directly impacted by the trauma (Outland et al., 2020).

In conclusion, the team facilitated a second project of phase II in 2019, which is reflective of this book. However, prior to presenting information from this work, readers must first understand the problem of police killings of youth victims, and in turn, become aware of the rationale and purpose for this caliber of critical research. This information, along with an introduction to *Deputized Violence*, is provided in the following sections.

Police Terrorism of Youth and Their Communities With Impunity

In the United States of America, police killings of citizens remain an ever-pressing epidemic. For instance, for nearly a decade, 1,000s of citizens have lost their lives to police or law enforcement violence in the United States of America (Mapping Police Violence, 2022). Many victims who were killed during this period were unarmed, struggled with mental health challenges, or resided in poor living conditions. Thus, being Black, poor, or struggling with mental health challenges can lead to a death sentence when encountered by police or armed extensions of state power (Abu-Jamal, 2016; Rodriquez, 2023). In this country, most police killings of citizens are state-sanctioned and *Justified*, which typically involves the police perpetrator being placed on paid administrative leave (i.e., paid vacation) while the police department performs its own internal investigation. Officers' performances during trial always suggest fear for their lives, granting them permission and governance by the state to act as judge, jury, and executioner in a given situation (Chaney & Robertson, 2013). Thus, the problem is clear: Police or law enforcement officers kill countless citizens each year with impunity (Halvorson, 2022) and most of these killings are deemed justified killings by the courts, returning these officers back to their posts in many traumatized communities (Bies, 2017; Schweikert, 2020).

Youth killings by police or law enforcement also remain a pressing crisis in U.S. society. For instance, in 2016–2017, more than 135 youth, victims' ages between 9 months and 19 years, lost their lives at the hands of law enforcement personnel. Majority of victims of these travesties were Black, Brown, and White males, with White females constituting the largest category of youth female victims of police killings (Outland, 2021). Furthermore, although these victims were children and teens and most were unarmed, a similar outcome remains: The officer involved was placed on paid vacation following the killing, only to be later found justified for his actions by the court. Thus, a grieving mother must exist knowing that the courts found the perpetrator of her child's untimely demise *Justified*, and at times, warranted, despite evidence that often leads to the contrary. Here, we see clearly that a major problem is that youth are also victims of police killings, which brings on major levels of confusion, betrayal, and deceit in their minds toward police according to the assumed logic that these state-sanctioned security forces are paid by working-class tax dollars to protect, serve, and *not* murder them (Smith, 2015; Staggers-Hakim, 2016). As a result, some may argue that citizens tax dollars in this country *are not* used to protect the well-being of youth, especially Black, Brown, and poor ones, but are used to further influence their untimely demise at the hands of police, or agents of the State; and in turn, blaming youth victims in the media for their *public death sentences* that were determined and issued by police.

Deputized Violence

The prevailing phenomenon of police terrorism of youth and adults has a major influence on the notion of deputized violence in the United States. *Deputized Violence* connotes the idea that police, law enforcement, and in some cases common citizens, are sanctioned by the state to take the life of another as long as the act occurs within the confines of the supposed law (Mowatt, 2022; Seigal, 2018). For instance, Qualified Immunity grants police officers credence by the State to kill citizens in scenarios where according to the officers' perception, they felt threatened, afraid, or assumed to be in danger (Obasogie & Newman, 2017). Furthermore, Stand Your Ground laws in many states also denote aspects of deputized violence by common citizens. In similar language as Qualified Immunity, Stand Your Ground laws grant citizens the right to use lethal force in scenarios where individuals perceive themselves and/or their private property as being threatened by others (Giffords Law Center, 2020). Indeed, all citizens must have the right to defend themselves and their property against possible external threats. However, a major problem with Stand Your Ground laws ensues once citizens decide to use lethal force in order to solve most, if not all, problems with others. For example, scholars discovered that Stand Your Ground laws do not create safety in the United States, but increase rates of homicide, primarily among White males (McClellan & Tekin, 2012). Furthermore, Stand Your Ground laws, according to Giffords Law Center, subsection of the Southern Poverty Law Center, tend to further exacerbate systemic racism and gender bias primarily in regard to who is mostly protected by the law when standing their ground (i.e., White males) when compared to victims of such law (non-White people – Huang, 2020; Giffords Law Center, 2020). Specifically, research suggests that "in Stand Your Ground states, these homicides were ruled justified in 45% of cases involving a white shooter and Black victim, but just 11% of cases involving a Black shooter and white victim" (Giffords Law Center, 2020, p. 10).

Thus, in a social context governed by Deputized Violence, citizens' use of lethal force to resolve social conflict with others becomes an inevitable outcome. Finally, forms of institutionalized violence also influence the notion of Deputized Violence. For example, jails and prisons (Jackson, 1971/1990), family separation at the U.S.–Mexico border (Chacon & Davis, 2006), and foreign wars and drone attacks led by U.S. forces (Abu-Jamal & Vittoria, 2018; Scahill, 2013; Seigel, 2018), all can be deemed as forms of Deputized Violence by the security apparatus (i.e., The State – Mowatt, 2022). As a result, Deputized Violence creates an illusion of placing the unchecked violence of the State in the hands of common citizens, which in turn, can lead to citizens becoming *purveyors of violence* with the intent that their acts will be supported, protected, and justified by the State (Seigel, 2018).

Deputized Violence by Police: Doctrine of Discovery and Manifest Destiny

In order to comprehend and make sense of *deputized violence* in the United States, there must first be an acknowledgment and discussion of the origins of this violence on these lands, which began centuries ago when the *agents* and mercenaries of European monarchies and imperialists invaded North America – what we now refer to as the United States (Dunbar-Ortiz, 2014). During these invasions, European mercenaries encountered Indigenous inhabitants of these lands and immediately devised unethical, treacherous, militaristic, and colonial plans to forcefully imprison and remove Indigenous peoples from the lands (Abu-Jamal & Vittoria, 2018). Of course, these European agents did not initially, upon arrival, engage in violent contempt of Indigenous folks, but rather devised deceitful plans to divide and conquer the diverse communities, tribes, and nations (Hill, 2010). The major theme, theory, and belief of the European monarchies and imperialists was the notion of the *Doctrine of Discovery*. According to the *Doctrine of Discovery*, any non-Christian lands west of Europe may be claimed for possession, given that the *people* inhabiting them were considered subhuman (Dunbar-Ortiz, 2014). Therefore, such imperialist ideologies precipitated and led to the deception, theft, plundering, rape, and genocide of Indigenous people by European settler-colonizers, along with their land and resources that continues today (Zinn, 1997). An understanding of this trajectory further contextualizes our discussion of structured, state-sanctioned violence, settler colonialism, colonization, and what we term, *deputized violence*.

Deputized violence consists of the structure and state, or monarchies and imperialists power and control over those they deem inferior, subhuman, non-Christian, and *different* (Mowatt, 2022). Thus, paving the way for what the imperialists refer to as *Manifest Destiny*. Manifest destiny in unison with the doctrine of discovery was the conduit and excuse implemented and practiced by imperialists to *conquer*, control, and colonize the Indigenous lands and territories of the Americas (Abu-Jamal & Vittoria, 2018; Hill, 2010). For these reasons, we must begin here, in our discussion and explanation of *deputized violence* as it pertains to current forms of state-sanctioned violence, which can include but not limited to police terrorism, policing, mass incarceration, poverty (everyday violence), and for so many others, known and unknown, *death*.

Book Overview

The overall purpose of this book, as previously stated, is to raise public awareness of police terrorism in the lives of youth and their families, primarily Black, Brown, and poor youth. If the general public is unaware that children and teens are also killed by police with impunity (Smith, 2015), then it is likely that we all will continue to denote police-involved homicides of citizenry as isolated occurrences, despite overwhelming evidence of this phenomenon remaining a national epidemic (Outland et al., 2020). Thus, in order to understand and combat state-sanctioned police violence, it is necessary for the public to take into account the historical purpose of policing in the United States, what purpose it served, and more importantly, the impact of its force, violence, and terror on citizens (Mowatt, 2022; Seigel, 2018; Vitale, 2018). This book entails the lived narratives of survivors of youth killed by police, which in many cases, loved ones of the deceased must embrace the social and emotional wounds of existing in close proximity to the officer following his return to active duty on the streets. In other words, acting as a symbol and extension of State power, the officer, the state-sanctioned agent of a youth's public death sentence, is a reminder of how the State protects its armed agents of unchecked violence, while simultaneously ignoring the suffering of survivors (Mowatt, 2022).

In the following sections, we attempt to review important literature surrounding the origins and history of policing, primarily in the United States. We further attempt to highlight police killings of U.S. citizens in recent times, especially in regard to deceased children and teens. According to research, 1,000 U.S. citizens on average were killed by police over the last decade, with some of the highest rates occurring in 2022 (Mapping Police Violence, 2022). Furthermore, 100s of children and teens were casualties of police violence over the last five years (Outland, 2021), while their families and loved ones are left to survive and endure these atrocities. Thus, the impact on survivors following the police killing of a youth, historically, has been under-researched. This book attempts to contribute to our collective understanding of what happens after police take the life of a youth, and the ways people who love the child are impacted. The narratives of survivors, activists, community members, friends, and law enforcement personnel who were impacted by the youth's untimely death can provide relevant information related to the social and public health epidemic of police terrorism in the United States, and the necessity for all people who care to critique, analyze, and eventually, transform this decrepit social condition. Yet, dismantling state-sanctioned violence by police carries a greater charge for activists and freedom fighters than simply calling for "police abolition" or "defunding the police," which remain foundational strategies to reduce police political and economic power (Seigal, 2018), as well as militarization (Kraska, 2007). However, the police remains the strong arm of the State, and when summoned, are permitted to use authority, force, and violence on Black, Brown, Indigenous, and poor people, which such acts are typically Justified by State power (i.e., Judicial Court), rarely if ever considering the vulnerability and age of victims (children/teens – Mowatt, 2022). In this vein, adequately addressing police terrorism in the United States will take a serious analysis and conceptualization of how the police is designed to protect the agenda, assets, and rulership of the economic elite and State (Seigal, 2018), which in turn, carries the potential for all working-class U.S. citizens, at any given time, to become victims and survivors of police killings.

The book concludes with a discussion on what can be done by everyday citizens to support and Love survivors of youth killed by police. These survivors need time, space, and Love from trusted and supportive people to heal (Outland et al., 2020). Due to the complex trauma experienced by survivors following their loved one's sudden and untimely death (Baliko, 2008; Kristensen et al., 2012), a variation of economic, legal, social, and spiritual supports are necessary factors during the healing process. Thus, a process of reparation can act as a necessary remedy to assist survivors in healing in the aftermath of a loved one killed by police.

Furthermore, concluding sections of the book include an honest discourse on ways to combat police terrorism, using historical references. If police reforms, reducing funds to build police infrastructure, and changing policy "still" do not limit the number of citizens killed by this security apparatus yearly, then it is evident that these solutions are "ineffective" to adequately address the epidemic. To arrest, jail, and convict "one" police for the killing of a Black man (i.e., Derrick Chauvin, a former Minnesota police officer, convicted for killing George Floyd – (Faulkner et al., 2021) does not end, address, and/or transform police killings of youth or adults. While one officer goes to jail, 100s of others are granted paid vacation (work suspension with pay), internally investigated, and eventually, actions deemed Justified by the courts. Due to the ongoing legacy in the United States of Black Rage, as an appropriate response to police killings, being laundered and monopolized by reactionary activists and major corporations (Too Black, 2022; Too Black & Mowatt, 2024), convicting one officer only gets at the tip of the iceberg of police terror as an extension of State power, and in turn, having little to no impact to address or end this phenomenon.

Finally, limitations of this project, as well as solutions to address them, are discussed in the final sections of the book. Our aim was to develop a methodology, or blueprint, for future scholars, researchers, activists, and freedom fighters to use as we collectively support (Rodney, 1975), Love, and organize with survivors of youth killed by police. The methodology is far from perfect and remains a work in progress. Nevertheless, since the inception of this work, we noticed an absence of ***a single*** blueprint for researchers to explore, learn, and in turn, publicize the lived encounters of survivors of youth killed by police. Thus, we hope this book can assist concerned people to extend ourselves and efforts on the ground, in the streets, to understand this phenomenon, and in turn, work collectively to once and for all, put an end to police terrorism in the United States. In this vein, actions and strategies taken by the oppressed class or masses to end youth killings by police in the United States, based on their terms, strategies, and conditions, are also *Justified.*

References

Abu-Jamal, M. (2016). *We Want Freedom: A Life in the Black Panther Party.* Common Notions: Brooklyn, NY.

Abu-Jamal, M., & Vittoria, S. (2018). *Murder Incorporated: Empire, Genocide, & Manifest Destiny.* Prison Radio Prison Radio: San Francisco, CA.

Baliko, B. (2008). Survivors of loss by homicide: Opportunities for nursing practice. *Journal of Psychosocial Nursing, 46*(5), 26–34.

Bies, K. J. (2017). Let the sunshine in: Illuminating the powerful role police unions play in shielding officer misconduct. *Stanford Law & Policy Review*, *28*(1), 109-[vi].

Chacon, J. A., & Davis, M. (2006). *No One Is Illegal. Fighting Racism and State Violence on the U.S.-Mexico Border*. Haymarket Books: Chicago, IL.

Chaney, C. V., & Robertson, R. (2013). Racism and police brutality in America. *Journal of African American Studies*, *17*, 480–505. https://doi.org/10.1007/s12111-013-9246-5.

Charmaz, K. (2014). *Constructing Grounded Theory*. Sage Publications: London.

Coates, T. (2013). Trayvon Martin and the irony of American justice. *The Atlantic*. Retrieved on 1/12/2023, from https://www.theatlantic.com/national/archive/2013/07/trayvon-martin-and-the-irony-of-american-justice/277782/.

CRG323.org. (2024). Critical Research Group.

Dunbar-Ortiz, R. (2014). Chapter 11: The doctrine of discovery. In Dunbar-Ortiz, R. (Ed.), *An Indigenous Peoples' History of the United States* (pp. 197–217). Beacon Press Books: Boston, MA.

Fanon, F. (2004). Colonial war and mental disorders. In Fanon, F. (Ed.), *The Wretched of the Earth* (pp. 181–218). Grove Press: New York, NY.

Faulkner, A., Favakeh, D., & Bredemeir, H. (2021). Derek Chauvin convicted for the murder of George Floyd. *The Butler Collegian*. Retrieved on 1/1/2023, from https://thebutlercollegian.com/2021/04/49178/.

Giffords Law Center. (2020). "Stand your ground" kills how these NRA-backed laws promote racist violence. *SPLC Action*. Retrieved on 1/10/23, from https://www.splcenter.org/sites/default/files/_stand_your_ground_kills_-_how_these_nra-backed_laws_promote_racist_violence_1.pdf.

Halvorson, J. T. (2022). *The Impact of Police Unions on the Prosecution of Officers, Legitimacy, and Reform*. Southern Illinois University Carbondale, OpenSIUC: Carbondale. Retrieved from https://opensiuc.lib.siu.edu/gs_rp.

Hill, G. (2010). *500 Years of Indigenous Resistance*. PM Press: Oakland, CA.

Hill, M. L. (2017). *Nobody: Casualties of America's War on the Vulnerable, from Ferguson to Flint and Beyond*. Atria Paperback: New York, NY.

Hooks, B. (2003). *Teaching Community: A Pedagogy of Hope*. Routledge: New York, NY.

Huang, M. (2020). "Stand your ground" kills: A new report from Giffords law center and SPLC action. *Southern Poverty Law Center*. Retrieved on 1/17/2023, from https://www.splcenter.org/news/2020/07/31/stand-your-ground-kills-new-report-giffords-law-center-and-splc-action.

Jackson, G. (1971/1990). *Blood in my eye*. Black Class Press: Baltimore, MD.

Kaba, M. (2021). Whether Darren Wilson is indicted or not, the entire system is guilty, part III. In Kaba, M. (Ed.), *We Do This 'Til We Free Us: Abolitionist Organizing and Transforming Justice* (pp. 54–55). Haymarket Books: Chicago, IL.

Kraska, P. (2007). Militarization and policing: Its relevance to 21st century police. *Policing*, pp. 1–13. https://doi.org/10.1093/police/pam065.

Kristensen, P., Weisaeth, L., & Heir, T. (2012). Bereavement and mental health after sudden and violent losses: A review. *Psychiatry*, *75*, 76–97. https://doi.org/10.1521/psyc.2012.75.1.76.

Mapping Police Violence. (2022). *Database*. Reviewed and Retrieved on 1/12/23, from https://mappingpoliceviolence.org/?gclid=Cj0KCQiAq5meBhCyARIsAJrtdr50wA0FuRzvDKZ9_faC6z-SRch3Q0G9SckiAHu68Pg1FgMv4ceBxzMaAsBAEALw_wcB.

McClellan, C. B., & Tekin, E. (2012). Stand your ground laws, homicides, and injuries. *National Bureau of Economic Research*. Retrieved from https://www.nber.org/papers/w18187.

Mowatt, R. (2022). Chapter 4: The society and the city: The identification for violence. In Mowatt, R. (Ed.), *The Geographies of Threat and the Production of Violence: The State and the City Between Us* (pp. 234–36). Routledge: New York, NY.
Nakajima, S., Masaya, I., Akemi, S., Takako, K., & Konishi, T. (2012). Complicated grief in those bereaved by violent death: The effects of post-traumatic stress disorder on complicated grief. *Dialogues in Clinical Neuroscience*, *14*(2), 210–214.
Obasogie, O. K., & Newman, Z. (2017). Police violence, use of force policies, and public health. *American Journal of Law & Medicine*, *43*, 279–295. https://doi.org/10.1177/0098858817723665.
Outland, R. (2021). Why black and brown youth fear and distrust police: An exploration of youth killed by police in the US (2016/2017), implications for counselors and service providers. *Open Journal of Social Sciences*, *9*, 222–240. Retrieved from https://www.scirp.org/journal/paperinformation.aspx?paperid=108618.
Outland, R., Noel, T., Rounsville, K., Boatwright, T., Waleed, C., & Abraham, A. (2020). Living with trauma: Impact of police killings on the lives of the family and community of child and teen victims. *Current Psychology*, *41*, 7059–7073. Retrieved from https://rdcu.be/cbkti.
Rodney, W. (1969/1996). *The Grounding with My Brothers*. Research Associates School Times Publications: Chicago, IL.
Rodney, W. (1975/1986). *Marxism and African Liberation: Speech by Walter Rodney at Queen's College, New York, USA in 1975*. From Yes to Marxism!, People's Progressive Party: Georgetown, Guyana.
Rodriquez, D. (2023). Chapter 12: The obsolescence of 'police brutality': Counterinsurgency in a moment of police reform. In Cunneen, C., Deckert, A., Porter, A., Tauri, J., & Webb, R. (Eds.), *The Routledge International Handbook on Decolonizing Justice*. Routledge: New York, NY.
Scahill, J. (2013). *Dirty Wars: The World Is a Battlefield*. Nation Books: New York, NY.
Scheper-Hughes, N., & Bourgois, P. (2004). Introduction: Making sense of violence. In Scheper-Hughes, N., & Bourgois, P. (Eds.), *Violence in War and Peace: An Anthology* (pp. 1–32). Blackwell Publishing: Malden, MA.
Schweikert, J. R. (2020). Qualified immunity: A legal, practical, and moral failure. *Cato Institute, Policy Analysis No. 901*. Retrieved from https://papers.ssrn.com/sol3/papers.cfm?abstract_id=3694725.
Seigel, M. (2018). Violence works: Policing and power. *Race & Class: Institute of Race Relations*, *59*(4), 15–33.
Smith, J. R. (2015). Unequal burdens of loss: Examining the frequency and timing of homicide deaths experienced by young black men across the life course. *Research and Practice*, *105*(3), 485–490.
Staggers-Hakim, R. (2016). The nation's unprotected children and the ghost of Mike Brown, or the impact of national police killings on the health and social development of African American boys. *Journal of Human Behavior in the Social Environment*, *26*(3–4), 390–399.
Too Black. (2022). Laundering black rage. *Black Agenda Report*. Retrieved on 1/16/23, from https://www.blackagendareport.com/laundering-black-rage.
Too Black, & Mowatt, R. (2024). *Laundering Black Rage: The Washing of Black Death, People, Property, and Profits*. Routledge: London, UK.
Vitale, A. S. (2018). *The End of Policing*. Verso: New York, NY.
Zinn, H. (1997). *A People's History of the United States*. New York Press: New York, NY.

2

UNDERSTANDING THE HISTORY AND PURPOSE OF POLICING IN THE UNITED STATES

From Armed Resistance to an Epidemic of Police Killings

Part I: History

Policing in the United States: History and Purpose

To begin a critical and honest discourse on the history and purpose of policing in the United States, we must first extend its historical etiology to the state-sanctioned government extermination of the Indigenous people of Turtle Island. When European Colonizers first arrived at Turtle Island on October 12, 1492, Cristoforo Colombo stumbled upon the island of Guanahani (believed to be San Salvador), in the Caribbean region (Hill, 2010, p. 11), which historians remind us of the absence of state-sanctioned forms of policing, as well as jails and/or prisons on Turtle Island. For example, upon first encounter of the Taino Arawaks, the natives of Guanahani (whom he called "Indians" and of Asian descent), Colombo's own log speaks toward his own greed and of his European handlers. We must not forget that the notion of "enslavement of Indigenous" is alluded to in Colombo's statement, which can only take place vis-à-vis violent force. He states,

> No sooner had we concluded the formalities of taking possession of the island than people began to come to the beach . . . They are friendly and well-dispositioned people who bear no arms except for small spears . . . They out to make good and skilled servants . . . they can easily be made Christians, for they seem to have no religion . . . If it pleases you, Our Lord, I will take six of them to Your Highnesses when I depart.
>
> *(from Colombo's log, October 12, 1492 – Hill, 2010, p. 11)*

DOI: 10.4324/9781003665915-2

European colonizers arrived to a land and people who governed themselves according to the Laws of Nature and matriarchal government structures. "The political sphere of Indigenous life was not dominated by men, but was in many cases the responsibility of women" (Hill, 2010, p. 10). Moreover, communal and tribal governance, most often facilitated by elder women, provided many Indigenous tribes practical strategies for problem-solving and dealing with social conflicts. For instance, "there were no prisons . . . the first Nation peoples had well developed methods of resolving community problems . . . community decisions were most frequently made by consensus and discussions amongst the people" (Hill, 2010, p. 10). As a result, communalism and matriarchal tribal structures allowed Indigenous people a governing system to deal with one another without the ensuing practices of "Crime and Punishment," which at the time, were all too frequent in European countries (Hess, 2000). Specifically, Penny Hess (2000), in her seminal work, *Overturning the Culture of Violence*, informed readers of the utility of citizens' taxes, prisons, and the police as tools to maintain social control and power between the working class and the ruling monarchy in Europe. Thus, when a common worker was unable to pay the weekly tax, the police would perform their designated duties to escort the citizen to the local jail or dungeon. Police further acted as a security apparatus around the living quarters of the ruling monarchy, which the police's primary purpose was to protect the property, assets, and lives of the few ruling elite from the working poor. In this regard, policing as an institution was not an origin of the Indigenous people of Turtle Island, but derived from the social, political, and economic unjust practices of the ruling monarchy of European countries (Hess, 2000, pp. 28–31).

Furthermore, the etiology of policing has its roots in the original European settlers' search for raw resources, primarily gold. Gord Hill (2010), in his powerful piece titled *500 Years of Indigenous Resistance*, suggests that the Indigenous people of Turtle Island welcomed European travelers with open arms and were willing to teach them their ways of life, which entailed living in connection to Nature and the Ecology. The Indigenous taught the visitors how to grow food, clean themselves, fertilize human waste, and live as one with the animal kingdom. The Indigenous were clear that they did not own Turtle Island, but simply shared its space and resources with those who dwelled on it. However, a challenge for European colonizers remained: They were only immune to being ruled by a monarchy, in which taxes, money, and an economy governed by state-sanctioned violence (i.e., policing and security apparatus) were the rule of the day. Thus, European colonizers' ambitions and lust for power became clear: To control the resources, primarily gold, as well as the land of Turtle Island. As we know, these ideas

FIGURE 2.1 African captives fight against an 18th-century slave ship crew. Captives greatly outnumbered the ships' crew and rebellions occurred on about 10% of slave voyages. Engraving from late 19th century.

can be promoted by some; yet, they are only implemented through force, violence, and policing. Thus, policing the Indigenous people was at the cornerstone of European colonizers' settlement on Turtle Island.

In addition, police were used to maintain the forced labor, or slavery, of Indigenous people by European colonizers. Specifically, since European colonizers were from a distant land and could not navigate the land, rivers, mountains, and mines for Indigenous resources, they forced the natives into bondage as chattel property to escort them to destinations that possessed resources. Thus, Indigenous natives were worked to the bone and death in many instances inside gold mines by their European colonizers. For example, during Colombo's four voyages to Turtle Island and the Caribbeans, remaining two in 1498 and 1502, including Trinidad, Panama, Jamaica, Venezuela, Dominica, and other islands, native peoples were captured by him for

> slavery and extorting gold through a quota of a hawk's bell of gold dust to be supplied by every Native over the age of 14 every 3 months . . .

> which failure to pay could result in cutting the "violators" hands off and leaving them to bleed to death.
>
> *(Hill, 2010, p. 13)*

Moreover, hundreds of Carib and Arawak were shipped to Spain as slaves under Colombo's governorship, 500 alone following his second voyage. Since Colombo was unsuccessful in finding the exponential gold he so often obsessed about, he decided to exchange the native Carib people "as slaves against livestock to be provided by merchants in Spain" (Letter to Queen Isabella; Hill, 2010, p. 11), or chattel enslaved workers.

According to Hill (2010), Colombo died in 1506 but his legacy as a European colonizer lived on. Specifically, "wave upon waves of first Spanish, then Portuguese, Dutch, French, and British expeditions followed, carrying with them conquistadors, mercenaries, merchants, and Christian missionaries" (p. 13). Furthermore, *Manifest Destiny and Doctrine of Conquest* by the United States and Western countries were historically supported, condoned, and encouraged by the Catholic Church and the Pope (Abu-Jamal & Vittoria, 2018). Specifically, one year after Colombo's first voyage, Pope Alexander VI, in his *Inter Cetera Divina Papal Bull*, granted Spain all the world not already possessed by Christian states, excepting the region of Brazil, which went to Portugal (Hill, 2010, p. 13).

FIGURE 2.2 Old illustration of Central American native warriors waiting for ambush.

As was the case in African Chattel Slavery by European Colonizers, slavery of Indigenous people was not only for work in mines but also for export to work as enslaved people in Europe. For instance, "in Nicaragua alone, the first ten years of intensive slaving, beginning in 1525, saw an estimated 450,000 Miskitu and Sumu peoples shipped to Europe . . . tens of thousands perished in the ships that transported them" (Hill, 2010, p. 16). Furthermore, Giovanni Caboto Motecataluna (John Cabot) kidnapped three Micmacs during his conquest across the Atlantic Coast of North America, which was financed by England, under the commission of Henry VII. In addition, Gasper Corte Real, financed by Portugal, kidnapped 57 Beothuks to be sold as slaves in order to "offset the costs of the expedition" (Hill, 2010, pp. 14–16). We must be clear that this can be identified as the original forms of slavery on Turtle Island.

As state-sanctioned violence works, European colonizers were only able to force the Indigenous people into physical subjugation as chattel due to terror, violence, and more importantly, policing (with weapons). Thus, policing, as an established institution, derived during the original settlement of European colonizers, which became evident during their search for raw materials and resources, primarily gold. According to this etiology, the primary purpose of policing was to enforce the slave labor of Indigenous people by European colonizers, while ensuring their free labor as escorts and miners of raw minerals and resources (i.e., gold). A European historian, as stated by Hess (2000), reminds us that since the Vikings, "piracy, or taking of resources through violence, brutality, and ruthlessness" (p. 21) by European colonialism had made its mark on Africa, Asia, and America. The goal: Europe's barbarous assault on world civilization was to culminate in the complete expropriation of the life-giving resources and labor of the peoples of the world for the benefit of White people. This is a relationship that could only be maintained by constant violence and economic dependency imposed by the oppressors (Hess, 2000, p. 21).

Thus, to the Indigenous, the role of policing, historically, is quite clear:

> In a 100-year period, the populations of the Indigenous peoples declined from 70–100 million to around 12 million. The Aztec nation had been reduced from 30 million to 3 million in one 50-year period. The only term which describes this depopulation is that of Genocide: an American Indian holocaust.
>
> *(Hill, 2010, p. 17)*

Policing and African Enslavement in the United States

Despite the label, name, etc., extended to the institution that carried out the duties of policing during the capture, imprisonment, and in turn, enslavement of Africans in America, conclusions can be drawn surrounding the purpose of policing. Specifically, of the more than 50 million Africans violently stolen and captured from our homeland, a large percentage (15 million) were brought to the Americas on scientifically engineered ships as captives, the African Holocaust and Middle Passage was directed, protected, and governed by a security apparatus. For instance, "15 million Afrikan peoples would be brought as slaves to the Americas by 1800, and a further 40 million or so perished in the transatlantic crossing in the miserable conditions of the ship's hold" (Hill, 2010, p. 16). This security apparatus consisted of smaller units or individuals who fulfilled the mandates of their rulers, to protect the assets and property of their masters. In this case, property was deemed as chattel or human life (stolen Africans by European slavers) in bondage in foreign and unknown lands. Overseers who subjugated African prisoners to rape, violence, and genocide on plantations (Abu-Jamal & Vittoria, 2018; Roberts, 1997), those maintaining social and physical control of Africans on prisoner ships during the TransAtlantic Slave Trade (Rodney, 1982), as well as the individuals who were summoned to capture the rebellious runaway slaves (Vitale, 2018), can all be deemed in one way or another, as a form of police. For instance, a good example is the purpose of policing by bounty hunters, or a form of police summoned to capture and return runaway chattel to its slaver (i.e., African prisoners to plantation owners). Thus, bound by law and perhaps local and state governance, the bounty hunter's overall responsibility was the protection of assets and property, vis-à-vis a safe return of human chattel to a slaver, and back to human subjugation (Abu-Jamal, 2016; Vitale, 2018).

Following the so-called end of chattel slavery of Africans in America by the State, convict leasing of African prisoners for cheap labor by industrialists and former plantation owners became a new market of human exploitation. Douglass Blackman (2008), in his seminal work, *Slavery By Another Name*, chronicles a history in the United States during the mid to late 1800s, when Africans in America were continuously captured by police, law enforcement, or racist vigilantes and hauled to prison for fabricated crimes, only to be later warehoused and forced to work in deadly mines and zones for exploitative or no wages. In this arrangement, police served as a point of opposition within the African colonized community, to identify, criminalize, and arrest Black people for fabricated crimes (Blackman, 2008, pp. 39–56). In turn, law enforcers ushered Africans to prisons, and later, these prisoners were forced into slave labor by the institution or industry, along with the economic and political elite who controlled it (Vitale, 2018, p. 47). As seems to remain the case, the police's primary purpose during the period of Slavery By Another Name, or Exploitation of African labor and bodies by industrialists and former plantation owners, was to protect the assets, property, and at times, the interest (i.e., cheap or free human labor for maximum profits) of the ruling elite. Blackman (2008) provides the following summary of this arrangement by suggesting:

> The same men who built railroads with thousands of slaves and proselytized for the use of slaves in southern factories and mines in the 1850s were also the first to employ forced African American labor in the 1870s. The South's highly evolved system and customs of leasing slaves from one farm or factory to the next, bartering for the cost of slaves, and wholesaling and retailing of slaves regenerated itself around convict leasing in the 1870s and 1880s. The brutal forms of physical punishment employed against "prisoners" [by correctional officers or police] in 1910 were the same as those used against "slaves" in 1840 [by slavers or overseers]. . . . These were the tendrils of the unilateral new racial compact that suffocated the aspirations for freedom among millions of American blacks as they approached the beginning of the twentieth century.
>
> *(p. 8)*

Original Police Force: United Kingdom to United States

Alex Vitale, in his book titled *The End of Policing (2018)*, points readers' attention to the original police force in the United Kingdom (UK) and the United States to establish an overall purpose for policing. For example, the *London Metropolitan Police*, also known as the "Bobbies," were established in 1829 by Sir Robert Peel. In search of new forms of social control that permitted the continued political and economic domination of the Irish by the British amidst growing insurrections, riots, and political uprisings, Peel, as manager of the British Colonial Occupation, developed the Bobbies with the core aim of not fighting crime, but "managing disorder and protecting the propertied classes from the rabble" (Vitale, 2018, p. 35) or poor working class. Furthermore, Peel later developed the *Peace Preservation Force (PPF)*, as a result of colonial expansion that reduced the military's ability to repress and eliminate mass uprising and resistance in Ireland. The PPF served two primary purposes: to manage crowds by immersing themselves in the resistant context (i.e., counterintelligence) and to identify and neutralize organizers of resistance via arrests and threats. Finally, *the Royal Irish Constabulary (RIC)*, acting as the primary urban police in Ireland for a century, was organized with the intent to maintain British rule and an oppressive agricultural system that produced widespread poverty, famine, and displacement (Vitale, 2018, p. 35).

Furthermore, a major turning point that influenced the original police force in the United Kingdom was the 1819 Waterloo Massacre. Specifically, in central Manchester, August 1819, thousands of people gathered to demand the end of widespread poverty and displacement due to industrialization. A cavalry charge with sabers, or special security forces, was summoned and killed a dozen protestors and injured hundreds of others. As a result, the London Metropolitan Police was formed by Peel, which "the main function of the new police . . . were to protect property, quell riots, put down strikes and other industrial actions, and produce a disciplined industrial workforce" (Vitale, 2018, p. 36). The London model was transported to Boston, MA in 1838. As a result of the widespread displacement and experienced poverty among European immigrants in search of freedom and liberty in the new world (U.S.), Boston experienced a chaotic economic and political context. For instance, the Broad Street Riot occurred in 1837, which included a "mob of 15,000 attacking immigrants" (Vitale, 2018, p. 37). Thus, local government called 800 cavalry to repress the mob of immigrants, and acting Mayor, Samuel Elliot, along with economic and political leaders, moved to forge a professional civilian police force (Vitale, 2018, pp. 35–37).

New York developed a larger and stronger police force in 1844. Similar to Boston, New York further experienced waves of immigrant uprisings to labor exploitation by capitalists, and Blacks and Whites united to demand economic transformation. For example, dock workers partook in sabotage actions in 1802, 1825, and 1828. Due to mass displacement, skilled workers further held strikes in New York in 1809, 1822, and 1829, which led to the founding of ten-hour workdays and establishment of the General Trade Union in 1833. These events, along with the Christmas riots of 1829, marked important turning points that produced the formation of the police of New York. Furthermore, it becomes clear that in this context, the primary purpose of police was to repress uprisings of immigrants and union workers in order to maintain labor exploitation and wage theft of workers by capitalists. In this vein, the purpose of policing was to protect the interest of the ruling elite, and not to protect and keep safe common citizens and workers (Vitale, 2018, p. 37).

The origins and purpose of the Chicago police were grounded in practices to repress and arrest newly arrived migrants from Europe. For instance, White Protestants, who were primarily Catholic, uneducated, and embraced racist ideologies, were concerned with controlling the moral and social behaviors of recent migrants. Such behaviors included, but not limited to, drinking, gambling, and prostitution. As a result, Law and Order Party Mayor Levi Boon established the first special police force in 1855 with the sole purpose to enforce "nativist morality laws." In addition, following an attempt by a group of German freedom fighters to liberate several dozen shopkeepers who were arrested due to such laws, known as the *German Beer Riots*, a city council called for more professional policing. This formation led to the establishment of the first professional police in Chicago, IL (Vitale, 2018, p. 38). As we see here, nativist moral laws established by the political order permitted disruption, repression, and isolation of new migrants, which in turn, the newly established police force's primary intent was to enforce such laws. In doing so, police corruption, violence, and spying became mainstream practices of the newly established Chicago police. Vitale (2018) reminds us,

> The extent of police corruption was so great that business leaders, journalists, and religious leaders banned together to expose [police] corruption and inefficiency and demand that police both become more professional and more effectively crack down on crime, vice, and radical politics.
>
> *(p. 39)*

Deputized Violence: Manifest Destiny and Doctrine of Discovery

As briefly discussed in the introduction of the book, *Deputized Violence* represents both literal and symbolic practices of state-sanctioned violence. *Deputized violence* is the idea and practice that agents (e.g., police and law enforcement) of the state, and in some cases common citizens, are appointed and delegated authority to act as a substitute for another or others, or represent a constituency in order to reinforce structured violence. According to scholars and historians, such as Ida B. Wells, W.E.B. DuBois, Roxanne Dunbar-Ortiz, Ralph Ginzburg, and Isabel Wilkerson, *Whiteness* itself was deputized in the United States, which represents a component of structural violence (Du Bois, 1935). From fugitive slave laws and codes to the protection of the exploitative capitalist economic system and Whiteness, deputized violence was used to *control* the formerly enslaved as chattel, suppress labor rights of the working class, and defend manifest destiny for the powerful, wealthy, and elite structures and agents of the system (Burden-Stelly, 2023). For example, the arming of newly arrived indentured servants to the colonized Americas (Hill, 2010), the genocide and oppression of Indigenous peoples (Dunbar-Ortiz, 2015), and the kidnapping and human trafficking of African peoples and their descendants (Hess, 2000; Rodney, 1982) are literal and symbolic practices of structural violence. Thus, structural violence provides the landscape, license, and tools for deputized violence. Deputized violence can be understood as reactionary violence toward others to *defend* self or property regardless of the threat level from others. In addition to defending self or property from threats of others, deputized violence may also be used to enact fear, control, and power over others. Thus, structural violence stems from a much larger system of operation, control, and expansion, where imperialists, monarchies, and representatives of papal influence and power shaped, indoctrinated, and directed plans for growth and the capture of land and people (Abu-Jamal & Vittoria, 2018; Bennett Jr., 1965; Dunbar-Ortiz, 2015; Vitale, 2018).

Notably, deputized violence represents a component of structural violence. According to some scholars, the roots of structural violence stem from the Second Amendment (Bennett Jr., 1965; Dunbar-Ortiz, 2015) – *a well regulated militia, being necessary to the security of the free State, the right of the people to keep and bear Arms, shall not be infringed* – essentially to *protect* the State, colonial powers, and settler colonialism. However, the origins of the Second Amendment date back to ancient Roman times and 16th-century England, where *Queen* Elizabeth I instituted a national militia which legally required all individuals, regardless of class, to defend the monarchy or empire (Charles, 2025). Initially, the narrative surrounding the Second Amendment in the context of the newly formed colonies and territories guaranteed the right of colonial settlers in the so-called *Americas* to *defend* the *Republic* against enemies both foreign and domestic (Abu-Jamal & Vittoria, 2018). With this in mind, it is equally important to highlight those considered domestic enemies of the *State* for which the Second Amendment applies. For example, Indigenous peoples and communities, and people of African descent who were imprisoned and *enslaved*. This includes the enforcement of *legal* yet deceitful and coercive treaties and agreements between the colonists and Indigenous people and the creation and enforcement of *Fugitive Slave Laws* (Bennett Jr., 1965; Hill, 2010; Vitale, 2018).

The Second Amendment, along with the Doctrine of Discovery, encouraged and legalized the right for colonial settlers to protect *their* land, themselves, and the government from enemies determined by the State. The Doctrine of Discovery and the Second Amendment called for land theft, while simultaneously and ironically calling for the *protection* of the land from Indigenous communities by arming settlers – establishing colonial and state militias – the national guard (Dunbar-Ortiz, 2015). In effect, this created a culture and more importantly, a *legalized system* where colonial settlers used *discovery*, violence, intimidation, and coercion in the theft of land and against Indigenous and formerly enslaved people. Consequently, this *culture* and legalized system were planted and harvested into what we refer to as deputized violence, a component of structured violence.

Unfortunately, what is much-less discussed is that in 1792, Secretary of State Thomas Jefferson claimed that the Doctrine of Discovery was *international law* that applied to the newly formed U.S. government. Interestingly, according to Dunbar-Ortiz (2015) this "international law" that Jefferson claimed applied to the United States was implemented in 1823, when the U.S. Supreme Court – led by Chief Justice John Marshall – held:

> The Doctrine of Discovery had been an established principle of European law and of English law in effect in Britain's North American colonies and was also the law of the United States. The court defined the exclusive property rights that a European country acquired by dint of discovery: Discovery gave title to the government, by whose subjects, or by whose authority, it was made, against all other European governments, which title might be consummated by possession.
>
> *(pp. 199–200)*

For this reason, Dunbar-Ortiz (2015) states that "European and Euro-American 'discoverers' had gained real-property rights in the lands of Indigenous peoples by merely planting a flag" (p. 200). What is of equal importance is that the courts did not stop there. They further asserted, "Indigenous rights to complete sovereignty, as independent nations, were necessarily diminished. Indigenous people could continue to live on the land, but title resided with the discovering power, the United States" (p. 200); "a later decision," according to Dunbar-Ortiz (2015, p. 200), concluded that Native nations were "domestic, dependent nations" (p. 200). The claiming of land by the U.S. government and its agents reinforces the beliefs and practices of structural and deputized violence perpetrated against Indigenous peoples, their lands, their homes, and their communities. By structuring *legal* arguments and documents that bolstered capitalist and religious ideologies and provided a foundation for the practice of land theft, oppression, and genocide of Indigenous peoples, the United States crafted, fostered, and practiced deputized violence.

Furthermore, in understanding how the Doctrine of Discovery and the Second Amendment further extended their claws and daggers into withholding the freedom and self-determination of Indigenous and formerly enslaved African peoples, we offer an additional compelling example. In *Before the Mayflower*, historian Lerone Bennett Jr. describes *slave codes*, which were "designed to keep slaves ignorant and in awe of white power" (Bennett Jr., 1965, p. 93). More specifically, these provisions forbade the formerly enslaved from meeting in "groups of more than five or seven" (p. 93) when not on their home plantation. They were banned from free movement and from passing off the plantation and from plantation to plantation, unless they were escorted by White persons and/or traveled with documents that *proved* they were *free*. According to Bennett Jr. (1965), "the presumption in most slave states was that a colored person was a slave" (p. 93). For this reason, Bennett states that "slave patrols or 'paderollers,' as the slaves called them, were authorized to make periodic searches of slave cabins and to chastise bondsmen found off plantations without passes" (p. 93). Equally important were other codes that "forbade slaves to raise their hands against whites and gave every white person *police power* over every Negro, free or slave" (p. 93). These codes and provisions, *mostly* in slave states, were not only orchestrated and enforced by slavers but reinforced by the "police power of the state, the militia, and the U.S. Army" (p. 93). Moreover, these physical acts of violence were also accompanied by psychological and emotional terror. Bennett Jr. (1965/2016) explains,

> More was needed; the slave, if slavery were to be successful, had to believe he was a slave . . . Each slave was taught, by various methods and with varying success, that he was totally helpless and that his master was absolutely powerful (p. 93).

Bennett Jr. (1965/2016) continues, "Each slave was taught that he was inferior to the meanest white man and that he had to obey every white man without thinking, without questioning" (p. 93). Bennett Jr.'s descriptions and insights present several independent yet intersecting philosophies and practices of structural and deputized violence.

To clarify, in order to describe and conceptualize the framing of, and approach to, structural and deputized violence, two fundamental and crucial points must be discussed. First, *structural violence* represented by the U.S. government was enforced long before the formal organization of police departments and governmental agencies (e.g., FBI and CIA), intrusive violations of treaties, and all other forms of symbolic and literal violence and terror. Second, *deputized violence* is a form of structural violence, which we argue is nestled or umbrellaed underneath and within *structural violence*. Thus, we define deputized violence as a tool of structural violence that endorses, legislates, implements, and authorizes agents of the state, or government, to exact and practice both emotional and physical violence and terror against *enemies* (i.e., Black and Indigenous bodies) of the State. In defining deputized violence, it is important to highlight that the State deputizes (mostly) White bodies and those who acquiesce to the rules of imperial colonization and settler colonialism, fueled by Manifest Destiny, greed, human trafficking, and the Second Amendment to act on its behalf when engaging non-White people on behalf of the State.

Moreover, Bennett Jr. (1965) and others provide vivid examples of the physical, emotional, and psychological violence perpetrated against people of African descent, Indigenous peoples, and non-White peoples. The codes, provisions, and policies enacted and practiced by the United States government and its agents (i.e., the *so-called* White citizens and settlers) indicate that these acts of terror and violence were not only independently practiced by people but were also fostered by imperialism and colonization of Indigenous land in the *so-called* America. Simply put, the U.S. government and its agents practiced, and continue to practice, structural and deputized violence against non-Whites and the White proletariats. In fact, the utility of deputized violence is reflected in the State's need for agents to carry out and enforce imperialism, colonization, and genocide in the colonies and eventually the *United States of America*. Certainly, Dr. Mutulu Shakur (2011), in his work with the *Truth and Reconciliation Commission* addresses the topic of deputized violence directly, he explains, "It must be understood that it doesn't have to be a complicit act by the whole government, but agents of the government can fulfill the obligation for culpability of crimes against humanity" (Shakur, 2011, p. 22).

Immunity With Impunity

While it is important to understand that the concepts and practices of deputized violence are rooted in Manifest Destiny, the Doctrine of Discovery and the Second Amendment are perpetuated by agents of the State, it is further important to highlight one of the major consequences of deputized violence: *Immunity* with *Impunity* or qualified immunity. Immunity with impunity represents *protection from*. . . and *exemption from*. . . Essentially, police officers and other *agents* of the State are permitted to carry out acts of abuse, misconduct, and killings, with no punishment; thus, the State protects state and local officials from liability, even when they act unlawfully and abuse their power, so long as their actions do not violate clearly established law (Baude, 2020; Schweikert, 2020). We recognize that several questions may emerge. First, what is qualified immunity and why is it important? Second, what are the origins of qualified immunity and what role does it play in structural and deputized violence, along with police and community interactions and relationships?

The doctrine of *qualified immunity* has shifted substantially over the past 50 years. The first and most notable case was decided in 1967 by the Supreme Court in *Pierson v. Ray*. In *Pierson v. Ray*, SCOTUS held that, because police officers *acted* in *good faith* during an arrest and that there was no previous analogous case to *Pierson*, they were in favor of the defendant (the police); however, there was an analogous case: *Myers v. Anderson*.

In the case of *Myers v. Anderson*, Maryland election officers denied Myers the right to register to vote, which was a violation of Section 1983 of the 14th Amendment (more on this later). The Maryland election officers claimed that because Myers could not prove that they acted maliciously or not in *good faith* they should not be held liable or accountable for denying Myers the right to register and vote. However, the court argued that *good faith* and malice were irrelevant in denying individuals their constitutional rights, nor could any State legislation overrule a constitutional one (Schweikert, 2020).

Both *Pierson v. Ray* and *Myers v. Anderson* cases stem from one component of Section 1983, of the *1871 Ku Klux Klan Act*, where Reconstruction Congress passed a series of three Enforcement Acts legislation to "combat lawlessness and civil rights violations in the postwar South" (Schweikert, 2020, p. 3) three years after the passing of the 14th Amendment. More specifically, Reconstruction Congress passed this provision to hold agents or parties "acting under state authority who cause the violation of a protected right liable to the party injured" (p. 3). This reconstruction era statute sought to hold agents of the state liable and accountable – while performing their duties – for terrorizing, injuring, and violating the protected rights of individuals. As a result, with this statute, Congress provided no immunity to agents of the State if they denied, injured, or violated the protected rights of people while performing their duties (history.house.gov; Mosvick, 2021; Schweikert, 2020). Given the rise in White racist vigilante violence and terrorism against formerly enslaved Africans, Indigenous people, and other non-White people post-Civil War, Congress passed the act so that agents of the state could not claim *immunity* while acting on behalf of the State. The act allowed for persons who were violently terrorized by agents of the state to seek damages against those agents without interference or protection from the government; thus, injured citizens could sue agents of the state for damages of their protected rights (history.house.gov; Mosvick, 2021; Schweikert, 2020).

Interestingly, this statue is the antithesis of how we understand qualified immunity currently. Over the past century, qualified immunity, or lack thereof, has evolved into protections for agents of the government in performing their duties, regardless of those actions or violations of citizens' protected rights. However, the utility of constitutional or protected rights is insignificant if agents of the State can violate these rights with impunity (Schweikert, 2020). As mentioned previously, Section 1983 of the 1871 Ku Klux Klan Act was revisited most popularly in the 1960s and 1970s when the Supreme Court of the United States found and argued in the *Pierson v. Ray* case that qualified immunity should be extended to law enforcement officials and any other agent acting on behalf of the State (Wright et al., 2022). Consequently, qualified immunity *allows* and *protects* law enforcement and any other agents of states or common citizens (e.g., vigilantes) to practice deputized violence in defense of the State and government. Therefore, we present qualified immunity as a deadly weapon that reinforces structural and deputized violence.

Despite what is presented in this work, much of what is cited stems from conservative legal scholars and researchers who are *pro* police. While they disagree with qualified immunity, some are ardent and unwavering supporters of police and the institution of policing/law enforcement and incarceration. In fact, conservative legal analysis of qualified immunity argues that the question of qualified immunity is immaterial if citizens' constitutional rights are not violated. One example offered by conservative legal analysts and scholars is that qualified immunity delegitimizes the institution of policing and law enforcement "by depriving officers of the public trust and confidence that is necessary for them to do their job safely and effectively" (Schweikert, 2020, p. 8). Moreover, conservative legal analysts and scholars provide examples from the Pew Research Center, where a survey of approximately 8,000 police officers found that 72% disagreed with the statement "officers who consistently do a poor job are held accountable" (Schweikert, 2020, p. 9). Interestingly, findings from a study at the Pew Research Center are parallel to the majority of the public who mistrust and have a lack of confidence in the police. The irony here is that if the majority of police officers do not believe that officers who consistently do a poor job are held accountable, then why should the public believe in or trust policing?

Nevertheless, this argument does not address the terror experienced by Black, non-White people, disenfranchised communities, and neighborhoods that are occupied and over-policed. The terror, murder, pain, and *ripple effect* leave victims, survivors, and communities oppressed and traumatized (Outland et al., 2020). With this in mind, it is of great importance to note that according to the Pew Research Center, approximately 60% of the public reported that "fatal police-Black encounters are signs of a broader problem" (Morin et al., 2017, pp. 5–6) while nearly 67% of police claim that these are "isolated incidents" (pp. 5–6). For these reasons, we conclude that the institution of policing and police terrorism/violence are fostered and insulated by qualified immunity – it is systemic, structural, and ***deputized violence*** that has historically and is currently, ***Justified.***

> Violence aimed at the recovery of human dignity and at equality cannot be judged by the same yardstick as violence aimed at maintenance of discrimination and oppression.
>
> *Walter Rodney, 1969/1996, The Groundings with My Brothers*

History of Radical Resistance to Colonialism, Slavery, and Police Violence

Indigenous Resistance to U.S. Colonialism and State-Sanctioned Violence

Throughout the 1600s and 1700s, during European Colonialism of Turtle Island and the Caribbeans, the settlers and mercenaries were always met with recalcitrant Indigenous resistance, primarily in lands that were yet to be invaded, stolen, and conquered by European forces, including Portuguese, French, and British. To understand the "why" surrounding Indigenous resistance to Colonial conquest of their land and resources, the following statement summarized Colombo and Western forces mission:

> The Duality of Colombo's mission, and the subsequent European invasions that followed, was the Christianization of non-Europeans and the expropriation of their lands. The two goals are not unconnected; "Christianization" was not merely a program for European religious indoctrination, it was an attack on non-European culture (one barrier to colonization) and a legally and morally sanctioned form of war for conquest . . . Even his name was prophetic to the world he encountered – Christopher Columbus translates to 'Christ-bearer Colonizer'.
>
> *(Hill, 2010, p. 12)*

Thus, Indigenous peoples' resistance to European settler colonialism began as early as Colombo's return to Hispaniola (today Haiti and Dominican Republic), which was deemed as the first settlement on Native lands by the colonizer and his voyagers. Specifically, in September 1493, he returned with a fleet of 17 ships and 1,200 men in which the detachment that had been left on Hispaniola was destroyed following outrages by the Spaniards against the Taino. In addition, Amerigo Vespucci (the Americas are named after) and Alonso de Ojeda were active raiders of enslaved people in the West Indies and South America's Pacific Coast. *Ojeda*, during a raid, was killed by a warrior's poisoned arrow for his efforts. Furthermore, in an attempt to land in Florida, Ponce De Leon, the navigator, was driven off by 80 Calusa war canoes. In 1543, although Pedro de Valdivia claimed Chile for the Spanish Crown, fierce resistance by the Mapuche nation restricted the Spanish to the northern and central regions . . . Valdiva was killed in battle by Mapuche warriors (Hill, 2010, pp. 12–14).

Furthermore, following the establishment of the Plymouth colony by Pilgrims in 1620, Beothuks in Newfoundland had retaliated against a French attack in clashes that killed 37 French settlers. The French retaliated by arming Micmacs, historical opposition to Beothuks, and in turn, *offered bounties for Beothuks scalps.* In identifying this process as the origin of scalp-taking by native warriors, it must be clear that this practice was "introduced and financed" by French settlers, which in turn led to the eventual extermination of the Beothuks (Hill, 2010, p. 19).

In 1622, while European settlers and colonizers fought for land and resource domination on Turtle Island, the Indigenous found themselves under constant attack. Thus, when a force from the Plymouth colony massacred a group of Pequots, the Pequot warriors attacked a settler village at Wessagusset. In 1622, the Powhatan Confederacy, led by Opechancanough, attacked the Jamestown colony, which was deemed as a serious threat to drive the colonizers back into the sea. In addition, clashes between the Powhatan Confederacy and European settlers continued, until Opechancanough was captured and killed. In 1655, the Delaware warriors attacked several Dutch settlements after a Dutchman killed a Delaware nation woman for picking a peach tree on the colony's "property" (Hill, 2010, p. 22). The Indigenous resistance lasted along the Hudson River until 1664. In 1676, the English arrested and executed three Wapanoags for the alleged killing of a Christianized Native, believed to be a traitor. The Narragansetts, Nipmucs, and Wapanoags, led by Metacom (also known as King Philip by the Europeans), rebelled against the New England colonies. Metacom was killed, and his family and hundreds of others were sold to slavers in the West Indies. Finally, in 1680, led by the Tewada medicine man Pope, the Pueblo people drove out the Spanish from Mexico (Hill, 2010, pp. 19–23).

Black Roots of Resistance to Slavery

Blacks, or Africans in the United States, have historically resisted European colonialism and our eventual enslavement in Turtle Island. History has shown that from the first attempts of colonizers to capture free Africans on the continent, the TransAtlantic human trade, along with the eventual establishment of the institution of chattel slavery, Africans in the United States have always resisted and fought ostensibly against their colonizers.

In his seminal work, *We Want Freedom: A Life in the Black Panther Party*, Mumia Abu-Jamal (2016) provided important historical depictions of Black Radical Resistance pre and post the American Revolution. He suggests that during the early 18th century, Africans were engaged in struggling for their right to freedom by capturing slave ships and returning back home, as well as organizing rebellions on foreign lands in Turtle Island. For example, 96 Africans aboard the *Little George* slipped their chains and overpowered the crew; despite some of the crew not being slain, those who survived were locked in cabins in order to not interfere with the journey back to Africa. Following a three-day voyage, they arrived on the West African Coast in 1730. Furthermore, two years later, the *William* vessel was captured by its African captives, which they slew the captain and set adrift the ship's crew, eventually "pointing the bow of the vessel homeward to Africa" (Abu-Jamal, 2016, p. 14).

Enslaved African rebellions to their capturers became "incessant" practices in Turtle Island during the 1730s and 1740s. Some historians have termed this period that of "the contagion rebellion," sweeping the colonies due to ongoing African resistance to slavery, or state-sanctioned and institutionalized violence. One historian noted,

> The following year witnessed rebellions in South Carolina, Jamaica, St. John (Danish Virgin Islands), and Dutch Guyana. In 1734 came plots and actions in the Bahama Islands, St. Kitts, South Carolina again, and New Jersey . . . In 1735–36 a vast slave conspiracy was uncovered in Antigua, and other rebellions soon followed on the smaller islands of St. Bartholomew, St. Martins, Anguilla, and Guadeloupe. In 1737 and 1738, Charleston experienced new upheavals . . . spring 1738. . . several slaves broke out of a jail in Prince George's County, Maryland, united themselves with a group of outlying [or escaped] Negroes and proceeded to wage a small-scale guerrilla war . . . In 1739, the Stono Rebellion convulsed South Carolina . . . slaves burned houses as they fought their way toward freedom in Spanish Florida.
>
> *(Abu-Jamal, 2016, p. 15)*

Furthermore, it must be noted that some 65,000 Africans joined the British cause during the American Revolutionary War. According to Abu-Jamal (2016), these Africans did not join the British cause in loyalty to the Crown, nor any disloyalty to the colony, but primarily due to an opportunity to gain their freedom through struggle. Specifically, Lord Dunmore offered freedom for any African willing to fight for the Crown, and tens of thousands of enslaved Blacks seized the moment. Black troops, also known as the *Ethiopian Regiment*, helped the British capture and torch Norfolk, VA on New Year's Day, 1776. Following the British's forced withdrawal in 1783, some 20,000 Africans fled the United States to settle in London, Nova Scotia, Ontario, and other British dominions (Abu-Jamal, 2016, p. 16). Ten years prior to Dunmar's offer, hundreds of Africans from the Spanish colony of Florida, primarily the Maroon communities from Fort Mose, decided to set sail for Cuba rather than exist under the British Crown. Fort Mose can be understood as the first Black settlement in the United States. As Abu-Jamal notes (2016), enslaved Africans were primarily concerned with living in freedom, rather it meant to join the British Crown against the U.S. slavers, or migrate to Cuba (Abu-Jamal, 2016, pp. 16–17).

Finally, post the American Revolution, enslaved Africans began to wage armed rebellions that struck at the heart of their capturers as well as the state-sanctioned institution of chattel slavery. Black freedom fighters of the 1800s, including Gabriel Prosser (d. 1800), Charles Deslondes (d. 1811), Denmark Vesey (d. 1822), Nat Turner (d. 1831), and "Cinque" Singbeh Pi'eh (d. 1839 – of the mutiny aboard the Spanish schooner *La Amistad*), are revered by contemporary Africans in America for their courage and willingness to organize free and enslaved Africans and White allies in order to wage armed struggle against their captives during one of the most brutal and dehumanizing periods of the United States. As Abu-Jamal (2016) noted, "Gabriel did not die to millions of his fellow captives. They still live on, in blessed memory, in spirituals, in legend . . . in the spirit of resistance of an oppressed people" (pp. 19–21).

Armed Self-Defense Against State-Sanctioned Violence and Police Terrorism

1800s Flight of the Maroons

History has demonstrated that in times of colonial violence and oppression, along with police terrorism and killings with impunity, oppressed groups, including Indigenous, Black, White, and Latinx people, have organized themselves for armed self-defense. This history of armed self-defense by oppressed groups against forces of colonialism began in the early 1800s flight of the Maroons on Turtle Island. The Maroons, consisting of a mix of more than 200 Black men, women, and children and approximately 30 Indigenous allies, lived in well-armed forts along the Apalachicola River, with a primary purpose to resist "attacks from whites (or Native Americans who hired them) who wanted to place them [Blacks] back in slavery" (Abu-Jamal, 2016, p. 21). Led by Andrew Jackson, Major General of the U.S. Army, the Negro Fort experienced a ten-day siege of the facility by U.S. forces. The siege concluded when cannon fire struck an armory causing it to explode, in turn, killing some 270 inhabitants (Abu-Jamal, 2016, pp. 21–22).

John Brown's Army

The 1859 siege of Harper's Ferry, West Virginia by John Brown and his cadre is worth noting amidst the history of armed resistance on Turtle Island. Specifically, as historians have recorded, among John Brown's possessions were

FIGURE 2.3 Washington, DC – September 12, 2023: Native American protestors at the White House call for the release of Leonard Peltier from federal prison where he has been incarcerated for 47 years.

a newly written *Constitution and Declaration of Independence*. Consisting of 48 articles and sharing similar elements as the U.S. Constitution, the newly written constitution was adamant and vehement in its rebuke and denunciation of the peculiar institution of chattel slavery. Thus, in a struggle not for concessions but for a free and liberated nation-state, Brown and his cadre seized Harper's Ferry with the primary intent to foment a mass slave revolt and to initiate an armed retreat to a redoubt in the nearby Allegheny Mountains in order to spark an ongoing harassment campaign of the system of chattel slavery. Although the plot was unsuccessful in its overall purpose, John Brown and this resistance became a symbol of struggle against slavery and White supremacy violence for centuries to follow (Abu-Jamal, 2016, pp. 24–26).

Armed Self-Defense During Civil Rights and Black Power Movements

Civil Rights Movement and Armed Resistance

Akinyele Umoja (2013), in his seminal work, *We Will Shoot Back: Armed Resistance in the Mississippi Freedom Movement*, provides important and informative depictions of armed resistance during this historical period. For instance, he reminds readers that armed self-defense and militancy were a natural part of organizing and movement building during the early stages of the Civil Rights Movement. These practices were deemed necessary due to ongoing racial and institutional violence practiced by Whites toward Black organizers and leaders. Furthermore, Mississippi Freedom Fighters, including Dr. Emmet Stringer, George Lee, T.R.M. Howard, and Medgar Evers, were among Black organizers and leaders who called for armed self-defense against the continued onslaught of racialized violence by the State and White racist vigilante groups. As members of the Regional Council of Negro Leadership (RCNL) or the National Association for the Advancement of Colored People (NAACP) of Mississippi, these Black leaders were not only committed to organizing Blacks for voting and other human rights, they were also deemed as respectable Black businessmen of their communities. Moreover, due to racial segregation by law and policies during the 1940s and 1950s, Black leaders and organizers were responsible for both providing basic necessities to the Black populace, along with security and protection.

Several examples of White supremacy violence and terror toward Blacks are noteworthy when considering "why" Black Freedom Fighters of Mississippi decided to defend themselves with arms, according to Umoja (2013). First, in the 1946 elections, the first statewide poll in Mississippi since *Smith v. Allwright*, White supremacists, including U.S. senator Theodor Bilbo, mobilized to prevent Black political participation. When considering the role and purpose of policing in this regard, "law enforcement officials and vigilantes physically attacked Blacks attempting to register as well as the small number of registered Blacks who attempted to vote in the 1946 election" (Umoja, 2013, p. 29). Thus, the goal of policing was not to protect and keep safe Black voters, but quite the opposite, which was to restrict their ability to mobilize and cast a vote for their respectable candidate.

Dr. Emmet Stringer

In addition, Black leaders, such as Dr. Emmet Stringer, president of the State Conference of Branches NAACP, were targets of economic intimidation by the State. For example, Dr. Stringer's wife was fired as a teacher from a Columbus public school. Moreover, Stringer experienced physical threats, as well as threatening letters and phone calls, which moved him to carry arms during his daily travels, at home, and at his work office (Umoja, 2013, p. 34). Media outlets, financial sectors, government officials, along with White racist vigilantes, collaborated to further repress Black Freedom Fighters of this period. Specifically, Dr. Stringer, along with George Lee, T.R.M. Howard, and Medgar Evers, were included on a list of nine key NAACP and RCNL activists published in the Delta newspaper and circulated to *The White Citizens Council (WCC)*. In coordination by the State and economic institutions (i.e., banks) of Mississippi, credit denial, nonrenewal of mortgages, and immediate demands of lingering debt were primary tools of economic intimidation used by WCC and its collaborators against these Black activists (Umoja, 2013, p. 34).

Reverend George Lee and Gus Courts

The ambush and murder of Reverend George Lee, RCNL vice president and local NAACP leader, in the streets of Belzoni, on May 7, 1955, was another example of White racist vigilante terror that moved Blacks to armed self-defense. Lee was suggested to be the first Black to qualify to vote since Reconstruction, an avid organizer of Black voting power, and known for his militant posture. After refusing to inform 30 Black Humphrey County residents to remove their names and vote from the poll, he received threats from local Whites and was eventually gunned down in the streets. Approximately 2000 gatherers attended his funeral, and Howard, amidst his grief and pain from the loss of a dear friend and comrade, reminded attendees that "We are not afraid. We are not fearful . . . Some of the rest of us here may join him, but we will join him as courageous warriors and not as cringing cowards" (Umoja, 2013, p. 34).

Several months following the murder of Rev. Lee, Gus Courts, an organizer of a contingent of Humphreys Blacks registered to vote and pay their poll taxes, was shot in his store by WCC members. Specifically, he was warned by the White racist group that he would be "next on the list to go," which in turn, he pleaded with the state government for protection. Rather than answering his request, his letter to the State for protection was given to members of the WCC, which they had in their possession prior to shooting him. He was rushed to a hospital two counties away by friends, due to concerns about the past care Rev. Lee received in Belzoni hospitals. Medgar Evers advised Gus Courts and his family to leave the state and provided an armed escort from the Delta to Jackson. Courts were forced to leave behind a $15,000 a year grocery business, home, and a legacy. Due to the federal and state governments' unwillingness to find the White vigilante terrorists who killed Lee and shot Courts, the Black Freedom Struggle realized their inability to rely on government forces for their survival and were convinced that they had to provide their own resources and protection (Umoja, 2013, p. 35).

As a result of the increased violent attacks on the Black Freedom Struggle, along with his increased militant activism, T.R.M. Howard became well known for his willingness to defend himself, his home, and to provide security and protection for the movement. For example, Howard was known by members of the movement to possess a cache of guns, pistols, and other weaponry. Moreover, he kept a pistol in a holster on his waist- and was known to carry a pistol in a hidden compartment while traveling in Mound Bayou of Mississippi. Security and bodyguards at his home and work office were common practices for Dr. Howard.

Dr. T.R. Howard and Medgar Evers

It is critical to note Howard's ability to provide shelter, security, and logistics support following the murder of Emmett Till. Specifically, two Delta White men, Roy Bryant and J.W. Millam, kidnapped, tortured, and lynched Till for allegedly whistling at Bryant's wife. His mangled body was discovered three days later in the Tallahatchie River (Umoja, 2013, pp. 36–37). Howard, Ruby Hurley, Medgar Evers, and Amzie Moore were active participants to disguise their identities (as a result of White racist terror), sift through the Delta, and assist in locating Till's body, which an active and armed security cadre was provided to protect the Black Freedom Fighters. Furthermore, Howard provided protection for several individuals involved in the Till case, including Till's mother, Mamie Till-Mobley. Howard's home was described as a "Black command center" and "haven" during Till-Mobley's travel, which he offered "protection, shelter, and hospitality for Mobley as well as Black dignitaries and journalists during the trial, including Charles Diggs" (Umoja, 2013, p. 37). Dr. Howard kept a security checkpoint at the front of his home, and Mrs. Till-Mobley was escorted to the trial in a "bulletproof" vehicle that was disguised with flower arrangements in the car to mask her true identity. Due to mounting threats of violence against the RCNL leader and his family, Dr. Howard was forced to flee Mississippi and sought refuge in Chicago, IL, which he eventually returned to Mississippi to assist in the escape of militant journalist Arrington High from a state mental health hospital (Umoja, 2013, p. 38).

Following the exile of T.R.M. Howard, Medgar Evers emerged as a vital figure of the Black Freedom Struggle in Mississippi that embraced armed self-defense. Specifically, Evers possessed background training and experience in military combat during World War II, which he and his older brother, Charles Evers, were discharged in 1945. Enlisting in the military as a sophomore in HS and leaving school to join the military the next year, Evers possessed youthful experiences with military training, which denote his militant posture and position toward self-defense as an adult leader of the Black Freedom Struggle.

Evers' initial confrontation with White supremacy threats of violence occurred in 1946. The Evers brothers, along with four other Black World War II veterans from Decatur, Mississippi, decided to register to vote. White supremacists got word of their actions and decided to impede the Black veterans' ability to vote by organizing some 15 armed White men "who prevented them from entering the building" (Umoja, 2013, p. 39). The Black veterans went home, armed themselves, and returned to the courthouse to proceed to register to vote. They were blocked by the armed White mob once again, and to avoid an armed war, the Black veterans decided not to pursue voter registration on this day. They were followed home by the armed White men, which the Evers brothers, Medgar as only a youthful teen, resided at their parents' place with armed security awaiting the return of the White racist mob. They never came.

Furthermore, Medgar Evers first received statewide and national attention when he attempted to register for Law School at the University of Mississippi (Ole Miss) in 1954. Evers' decision was influenced by the NAACP's legal challenge of school segregation, profound speeches by Dr. Emmet Stringer, as well as his belief in the need for legal expertise in the Civil Rights Struggle, such as NAACP attorney Thurgood Marshall. Thus, Evers went on to become the field secretary for the NAACP and was a major figure in organizing efforts to increase its membership in Mississippi from 874 to 1,481 from January 1954 to April 1955 (Umoja, 2013, p. 42).

It is worthy to note that Medgar Evers carried great respect and admiration for the nationalist struggle in Kenya. Specifically, the Kikuyu Land and Freedom Army, popularly known as the "Mau Mau," was an underground, peasant-based resistance movement that led a popular uprising between 1953 and 1956 in British colonial Kenya (Umoja, 2013, p. 42). Evers closely followed the Mau Mau struggle and had deep respect for the Black nationalist leader, Jomo Kenyatta. He shared with close friends and comrades the need for a Mississippi Mau Mau, which he envisioned would "retaliate against racist violence on Blacks" (p. 43). His goal: To utilize guerrilla warfare to bring national attention to the horrors of racial segregation in the Mississippi Delta. Although his ideas of a Mississippi Mau Mau were not supported by his NAACP fellows, who publicly espoused ideas of nonviolent resistance, Evers was well known for having guns and armed security in his vehicle, home, and during travels. For instance, his home was well protected by security detail, in which arms were placed across the street from the home, while other defense guards sat on the front porch to observe, identify, and respond to unfamiliar vehicles. Armed security was also organized to protect NAACP leadership and special guests, including NAACP President Roy Wilkins and Lena Horne, entertainer and friend of the Civil Rights Struggle. Moreover, the Evers' house was also protected by bulletproof blinds as well as a German shepherd. A week prior to Ever's assassination by White Supremacist, Byron De La Beckwith, the Evers family had received threatening phone calls and mail, and a "firebomb was tossed at their home in spring 1963" (Umoja, 2013, p. 47). On June 12, 1963, around midnight, Medgar Evers was gunned down by a high-powered rifle in his driveway after exiting the car. NAACP members observed De La Beckwith at a Jackson NAACP mass meeting the prior evening, where he sat with the media. For unknown reasons, Evers did not have a security detail or escort from the meeting to home, which some believed "he was supposed to have a bodyguard carry him home . . . I guess he got careless," according to Sam Bailey (Umoja, 2013, p. 48). Evers staggered from the car to his doorstep, where he collapsed. Houston Wells and other neighbors of the Evers family placed Medgar in a station wagon and covered him with a blanket, and transported him to a local hospital. He died shortly upon arrival.

Robert Williams

In concluding, the legacy of Dr. Howard and Medgar Evers demonstrates that Robert Williams' incorporation of armed resistance in North Carolina was no exception to the southern Black Freedom Struggle. Both Evers and Williams carried views and believed in the possibility of a "race war" and were prepared for armed struggle, and were less optimistic in the possibility of a peaceful integration between Blacks and Whites. Moreover, Williams was exiled in Cuba, China, and Tanzania due to the NAACP's contact with the FBI to investigate and charge Williams with crimes, which later forced him from the Civil Rights Struggle. During this period, Williams called for armed guerrilla warfare to protect Blacks from White racist violence and further embraced the "demands of the nationalist *Republic of New Africa* to establish an independent Black nation-state in the Deep South" (Umoja, 2013, p. 49). Thus, armed self-defense during the Civil Rights Struggle was about survival from White racist violence against Black freedom and human rights. Myrlie Evers, the wife of Medgar, suggested her husband stating,

> If white structural racism . . . was relatively "permanent," what practical options or alternatives did African Americans have? Perhaps Blacks should consider demanding a separate, all-Black state of their own, based on a territorial separation between the races . . . Medgar believed you must always be prepared for whatever comes our way . . . we were talking about guns, the arms, collecting what we need to fight if by chance we ended up in a race war . . . He was thinking about building a nation . . . of Black people.
>
> *(Umoja, 2013, p. 48)*

Black Panther Party

History reminds us that during the late 1960s, several Black, Brown, and Indigenous organizations utilized radical resistance, and at times arms, to combat police terrorism. A prime example was the Black Panther Party for Self Defense (BPP).

The formulation of the BPP occurred in late 1966 by Huey P. Newton and Bobby Seale, who had originally met at a political discussion at a local college. Newton's friend, Richard Thorne, introduced the pair during an Afro-American Association (AAA) meeting in spring 1962 and reacquainted two weeks later during a protest of the Kennedy Administration blockade of Cuba (Whitaker, 2023, p. 65). After becoming dissociated with the politics of student organizations on the college campus, they decided to develop a program that assisted, worked for, and spoke for the struggles of the people. In a two-week period of early October 1966, Huey and Bobby developed the ten-point program for the BPP. According to Seale (1991), Huey wanted to develop "a program for the people . . . that relates to the people . . . that the people can understand . . . that people can read and see, which expresses their desires and needs" (Whitaker, 2023, p. 59). Furthermore, framed around the tenets of "What We Want" and "What We Believe In," the ten-point program included principles to guarantee all Black people fair housing, equal employment, military exemption, and more importantly, "we want an immediate end to police brutality and murder of Black people" (pp. 59–61). As a result of this important principle related to putting an end to police terrorism and containment in Black communities, the BPP was committed in ideology and practice to protect Black communities from police killings. BPP programming included, but not limited to, FREE food, clothing, health care, transportation aid, and elder support, along with support for families of incarcerated individuals (Seale, 1991).

One of the first programs by the BPP was the Police-alert Patrols. Specifically, BPP members, armed with guns, tape recorders, cameras, and law books, would follow police around the Black community. When witnessing a Black citizen of Oakland being harassed, brutalized, or wrongfully stopped by police, BPP members would intervene, demonstrating the power of the people via the law and armed self-defense. In Mumia Abu-Jamal's (2016) seminal work, *We Want Freedom: A Life in the Black Panther Party*, he quotes Huey Newton with the following:

> With weapons in our hands, we were no longer their subjects, but their equals . . . We would ask the community members if they were being abused . . . Most of the time, when a policeman saw us coming, he slipped his book back into his pocket, got into his car and left in a hurry.
>
> *(pp. 67–8)*

Newton further suggests,

> By standing up to the police as equals, even holding them off, and yet remaining within the law, we demonstrated Black pride to the community in a concrete way . . . People constantly stopped us to say how much they respected our courage. The idea of armed self-defense as a community policy was still new and a little intimidating to them; but it also made them think. More importantly, it created a feeling of solidarity.
>
> *(p. 68)*

Here, several points are made clear as to why the BPP chose armed self-defense against police terrorism. First, they believed in the legal right to protect their lives and those of their Black and oppressed neighbors from police brutality. These practices were demonstrated by the BPP within the confinements of the laws of Oakland, CA. In addition, due to the oppressive history and social context of Blacks by White racist vigilantes and police, the BPP principle of armed self-defense can be further understood as a symbol of Black pride, or Black and oppressed people's willingness to stand up for themselves. Hence, the Black populace expressed a deep respect for the courage and bravery of the youthful BPP members.

Nevertheless, a posture of self-defense and programs designed to serve the basic needs of the community made the youthful organization and its members primary targets of government corruption, intimidation, and neutralization.

Black Liberation Army

During the late 1960s to the mid-1970s, several radical organizations embraced a militaristic, armed resistance approach to deal with police terrorism and brutality of Black, Brown, and Indigenous communities. For instance, the Black Liberation Army, initially established as the Black Underground, can be understood as a politico-military organization with the primary purpose to fight for the independence and self-determination of African people in the United States. According to Jalil Muntaqim (2020), in his untimely work titled, *We Are Our Own Liberators*, in late 1968 and early 1969, the BLA was first developed as the Black Underground armed-military unit of the BPP. During this period, the BLA aspired to build alliances and relationships with the oppressed Black masses across the United States and to form armed units and train in rural areas, along with establishing caches in several major cities (i.e., LA, Oakland, Detroit, Chicago, and Philadelphia). Between 1969 and 1972, the BPP came under major attack by the federal government, which is known as the *Counter Intelligence Program*

(COINTELPRO). COINTELPRO was intended to disrupt and neutralize the community programs and freedom struggles waged by organizations, such as the BPP, which were part of the Black Power and Civil Rights Movements of the 1960s and 1970s. The BPP was a major target of this neutralization. For example, Veteran BLA member Saffiya Bukhari (2010), in her seminal work titled *The War Before*, provided the following narrative of internal contradictions and fratricide manipulated by COINTELPRO that destroyed the BPP:

> By 1971 there was so much internal bickering in the Party and so much deviation from principles that there was a split. And while we were dealing with those internal contradictions and that fratricide, the government was making a move on us through the counterintelligence program, which they called COINTELPRO. We were not aware of it at the time. We did not know a lot of things we saw as internal contradictions were actually being manipulated by the government. And every little mistake that they saw was used and preyed upon.
>
> *(pp. 120–121)*

She goes on to suggest the organizational rationale for the evolution of the Black Underground, or the BLA:

> December 4, 1969, it culminated in the death of Fred Hampton in Chicago, in the same year, Geronimo Pratt was incarcerated in California, shootouts went on in New Orleans and Detroit – all across the country the Party offices were under attack . . . by being inside the offices and being sitting targets were not really defending ourselves, we were making it easy for them [police]. . . so it was decided to secure the offices, the Party, and the community workers by going on the offense, with the objective to defend and liberate the Black community and to make it possible for the political apparatus to continue.
>
> *(Bukhari, 2010, p. 121)*

By 1972, activities by the federal government created a major split between the acting leaders of the BPP, Eldridge Cleaver and Huey P. Newton. In turn, this feud, orchestrated by COINTELPRO, caused the BPP to split into two major factions. Due to factionalism and the split by the BPP, the BLA took a posture of defensive-offensive in the struggle for armed liberation (Muntaqim, 2020, p. 30). Despite the Black Underground becoming skilled in tactics of armed struggle, including bank expropriations and ambush attacks, in the late 1970s, the BLA was suggested to partake in many tactics and activities against police, law enforcement, or the FBI from late

1970 to early 1976. For instance, several officers were either shot or killed during this period. Moreover, several shoot-outs between BLA members and law enforcement personnel occurred. Further reports revealed the BLA's involvement in ambush attacks on police stations, prison escapes of captured BLA members, bank expropriations, along with bombings and explosives of police vehicles and headquarters. An important aspect of this ongoing war was the reality that by November 14, 1973, seven BLA members were killed in different shoot-outs with police; 18 others had been arrested (Muntaqim, 2020, p. 35). Alongside many BLA members being either killed or captured and thrown in prison by the State, by the mid-1970s, the BLA was also experiencing a major contradiction with White armed liberation formations against the Vietnam War. Specifically, by 1973–1975, the contradictions had reached a climax, and in turn, White armed liberation groups were unwilling to provide "meaningful materials and support to the Black Liberation Movement." As a result, the BLA was without an aboveground political and structural apparatus, while also being pursued by COINTELPRO, FBI, and police operations (Muntaqim, 2020, p. 38). These details are important to consider, which as a result, can be argued to have fueled the decimation of the BLA over time.

In sum, the BLA took a defensive-offensive posture toward police and state-organized terrorism, brutality, and harassment against poor people and the Black community (i.e., Structural Violence). This posture of armed self-defense by the BLA could have influenced a major decrease in the number of police killings of U.S. citizenry, primarily Black, Brown, and Indigenous people. Further statistical evidence is needed to support this claim. Nevertheless, the evolution of the BLA in Black communities could be understood as a symbol or reaction of resistance to police and state-sanctioned oppression. Since there is the reality that most, if not all, police killings are deemed *Justified* by the courts, the BLA can be further understood as an armed formation which created *real-life consequences* following police killings of Black community members.

Young Lords

Origins and History

The origins of the Young Lords transpired in January 1969. Nestled in El Barrio, or East Harlem, a group of Puerto Rican college students gathered to raise consciousness and better understand the conditions of Puerto Ricans. Over several months, different members came and went, and eventually the group was named *Sociedad de Albizu Campos* (SAC – Named after the Afro-Puerto Rican freedom fighter, *Pedro Albizu Campos).* Original members of the youth collective included Miguel "Mickey" Melendez and Juan Gonzalez (later became the minister of defense), along with the support of Pablo "Yoruba" Guzman (later became the minister of information) and David Perez. These members gathered in May 1969 to clarify the mission and purpose of SAC (Enck-Wanzer, 2010).

On June 7, 1969, the Young Lords Organization (YLO) was established and defined as "a street gang turned political in Chicago." (Enck-Wanzer, 2010, p. 3). The YLO possessed a diverse coalition of members, which included some from street gangs, photographers, and activists from El Barrio and Lower East Side. On July 26, 1969, the New York Young Lords were established and received an official merger from the Chicago chapter. Borrowing from the Chicago Chapter of YLO and Black Panthers, the primary objective of the New York Young Lords was to address change at the local level in their immediate community through "serve the people" programs (p. 3). These programs evolved from multiple traditions (including political and spiritual/religious) as well as practical public strategies (i.e., cleaning up garbage, testing for disease, and free medical clinic). The following statement denotes some of the programs established by the YLO, along with their purpose:

> The YLO directed their attention to making life better in the various Puerto Rican slums. They founded a lead paint-testing program in response to countless children being poisoned by the paint in their homes. They ran a blood and "x-ray" testing program for tuberculosis. They established community education initiatives, a breakfast program for poor children, free clothing exchanges, and day care for working families. They also led the drive to renovate a hospital (Lincoln Hospital in the Bronx) that had long been condemned for being unsanitary and unsafe, and they established the first in-patient drug rehabilitation program for the working class.
>
> *(Enck-Wanzer, 2010, p. 4)*

Due to YLO's commitment to political education and activism in the El Barrio, they acquired a broad membership of active organizers (ranging in the 1000s) as well as loyal nonmember community-based support.

The New York Young Lords split from the Chicago chapter in May 1970. Following the split, the New York YL became the Young Lords Party (YLP). According to Enck-Wanzer (2010), the YLO split was based on several reasons. These included differences in political views and opinions, NY chapter not receiving recognition from Chicago YL for work accomplished, and belief that Chicago's chapter had a hard time letting go of gang or street activity. This split led to YLP sharpening its political aim and vision for the organization, which fueled its expansion in Puerto Rican membership. They carried a creed that they involved "the Puerto Rican people wherever they [were] at any level of struggle" (p. 4). In addition, the YLP was divided into five distinct organizations. They included the *Puerto Rican Worker's Federation* (struggle for employment rights), *Lumpen organization* (organized rights for the unemployed, people incarcerated, drug users, etc.), *Women's Union* (struggle for women, gender, and sexuality rights), *Puerto Rican Student Union* (mobilized HS and college students), and *Committee for the Defense of the Community* (dealing with community issues including health, land use, and breakfast programs – p. 4). Speaking to a group of Hawaiian students in November 1971, Juan Gonzalez suggested that the YLP attempted to

> [b]uild a structure to involve our people in whatever level they wanted to involve themselves . . . . So, we see those people's organizations as the beginning, the seed of the people's self-government where the people train themselves to be involved in the revolutionary process and exercise their political power.
>
> *(Enck-Wanzer, 2010, p. 5)*

A telling story was the final phase of the Young Lords, which transitioned from the YLO, to the YLP, to the Puerto Rican Revolutionary Workers Organization (PRRWO). According to some authors, the focus of the PRRWO drastically shifted from community programs to "workers' struggle from an international Marxist perspective." As a result, Karl Marx, Friedrich Engels, and other communist theorists replaced iconic figures of Puerto Rican and African history, including Ernesto "Che" Guevara, Pedro Albizu Campus, and Malcolm X. Moreover, community offices and programs were dismantled, and a proto-authoritarian regime led by Gloria Fontanez evolved, in which some loyal members were beaten, placed on house arrest, or labeled spies or agents for COINTELPRO. The PRRWO would completely dissolve in 1976 (Enck-Wanzer, 2010, p. 5).

Young Lords and Armed Struggle

> Point 12 of 13. WE BELIEVE ARMED SELF-DEFENSE AND ARMED STRUGGLE ARE THE ONLY MEANS TO LIBERATION.
>
> We are opposed to violence – the violence of hungry children, illiterate adults, diseased old people, and the violence of poverty and profit. We have asked, petitioned, gone to courts, demonstrated peacefully, and voted for politicians full of empty promises. But we still ain't free. The

> time has come to defend the lives of our people against repression and for revolutionary war against the businessperson, politicians, and police. When a government oppresses the people, we have the right to abolish it and create a new one. ARM OURSELVES TO DEFEND OURSELVES!
>
> (Enck-Wanzer, 2010, p. 13)

Armed self-defense, according to the Young Lords, was a distinct feature of the organization. They defined armed struggle as a "constant offensive in the face of more men and more guns." The YLP believed in not provoking the enemy or becoming reactionary, overemotional in one's response to conflict, which placed the freedom fighter in a suicidal position. Moreover, they did not believe in a defense of being trapped in a building, but the idea of "offense is defense" (Enck-Wanzer, 2010, p. 142). The YLP believed that armed struggle was the "peak of a people's war," a phase signifying "the beginning of the end" (Enck-Wanzer, 2010, p. 144). They discussed armed struggle as a long, dreary road, which the oppressor fears the people's unity and ability to resist oppression. The following excerpt reflects this logic, which extends from the Palante newspaper (1970):

> The road to freedom is not an easy one – it's always getting harder. Somewhere along that road, the oppressor becomes afraid of our unity, of our growing strength. They become afraid because we are clear about our goals and they are unable to stop us. And the clubs start swinging, people start screaming, bullets start flying, sirens start blaring, tanks start rolling, and maybe bombs start falling.
>
> *(Enck-Wanzer, 2010, p. 151)*

Furthermore, the Young Lords discussed the gradual transition from political to armed struggle. They suggest this process as being fierce, and at times quiet, but little by little, eventually transforming into a full-scale war, experiencing casualties on both sides. They stated,

> It comes fiercely, sometimes, and quietly other times. And little by little, over a period of time, what had been mainly a political struggle, a battle of words, demonstrations, strikes, conferences, newspapers, becomes a battle with arrests, courts, hospitalizations, dead, wounded, orphaned, occupations, and retaliations. The political struggle begins to give way to the armed struggle. The political struggle frees the minds of the people, and the armed struggle frees the bodies of the people.
>
> *(Enck-Wanzer, 2010, p. 152)*

The Young Lords believed that the major purpose of a true revolutionary party was to "give guidance, education, and organization to the building of a people's party" (Enck-Wanzer, 2010, p. 152). According to this notion, this meant organizing for the future post armed-struggle and being prepared to navigate current and future conditions. The importance of a people's army, according to the Young Lords, provides the people a tool to ensure justice and to be prepared to defend themselves against the war waged "on us by the racist capitalists all our lives" (Enck-Wanzer, 2010, p. 152).

Two important Young Lord Casualties furthered their commitment to armed struggle over time. Specifically, on April 4, 1969, a Chicago police shot and killed Young Lord Manuel Ramos. The courts never tried the officer and the killing was deemed *JUSTIFIED.* A year and a half later, on October 16, 1970, correctional officers killed and hanged Young Lord Julio Roldan at *the Tombs*, a prison in New York City. As a result, on October 18, 1970, more than 2,000 people marched in Roldan's funeral procession, in which Young Lords and allies seized the People's Church for a second time with "arms, with shotguns, rifles, everything we could find, and prepared to defend it." At this stage, the Young Lords refused to allow police to gun down any more members and took the position to defend themselves. According to Juan Gonzalez, "The YOUNG LORDS PARTY was not going to begin shooting down police in the streets or bombing places. We are just going to defend ourselves from murder. And our people will do the same" (Enck-Wanzer, 2010, pp. 216–217).

Young Lords and the Red Squad: Police Infiltration

According to Jacqueline Lazu's (2013) seminal work, *The Chicago Young Lords: (Re) constructing Knowledge and Revolution*, she highlights the Young Lords' experiences of police surveillance and intelligence in Chicago, known as the Red Squad. Referencing Frank Donner's work titled, *In Protectors of Privilege: Red Squads and Police Repression in Urban America*, she described the red squad as "police intelligence units that specialized in overt and covert tactics, such as surveillance, infiltration and intimidation" (p. 42). She further suggests that the Red Squad's initial role was as henchmen for a machine-run workforce that targeted supposed "anarchists." Their repression focused on individuals and organizations that potentially hired communists (i.e., Red Scare) between the 1930s and 1960s and later expanded their repression to minority and reform organizations following the 1968 Democratic convention. The author reminds us that "YLO experienced not only full surveillance by the Red Squad but infiltration and constant arrest, which they identify as being ultimately detrimental to the organization" (p. 42). Furthermore, a major confrontation between YLO and Chicago police ensued during the spring of 1969. Following the police killing of Manuel Ramos, YLO members demanded a meeting with Cook County State's Attorney Edward Hanrahan. After Hanrahan refused the meeting, Young Lords organized a march and protest to the police station, drawing a crowd of more than 2000 people (p. 43). These activities, coupled with propaganda attacks against DePaul University for gentrification practices, drew the attention of well-known activists in the Chicago area, including Chairman Fred Hampton Senior and Huey P. Newton (*BPP Members, Chicago, IL and Oakland, CA, respectively*), along with the Brown Berets (Mexican activists) and Young Patriots (White organizing party). These groups eventually formed the Rainbow Coalition (Lazu, 2013, pp. 42–43).

American Indian Movement (AIM)

From its origin, the American Indian Movement (AIM) was founded on July 28, 1968 in Minneapolis, MN, by Dennis Banks, Clyde Bellecourt, and George Mitchell. All members stemmed from the Chippewa tribe of Minnesota. In addition, they were interconnected through past community service work as activists on an antipoverty program and social workers (Mitchell) in Minneapolis. Banks and Bellecourt met during their experiences in jail, which they believed influenced their commitment to Indigenous rights, primarily those from urban sectors. The primary purpose of AIM was to "address the problems faced by Indians in an urban environment. Racism and poverty created grave problems for urban Indians for which they were ill prepared to deal" (Schuttler, 1991, p. 20).

In August 1968, AIM members developed a list of objectives. AIM objectives were intended to create freedom and liberation for urban Indigenous people, with hopes of fully experiencing the "American Dream" in the United States. These objectives included short-term and long-term goals, which the former included housing, education, and employment rights and the latter entailed the unification of urban Indigenous people as a tool to dismantle and eradicate poverty and racism in urban Indigenous communities. Thus, with the latter goal's intent to forge and promote "pan-Indianism," AIM gained national attention based on this position, while simultaneously being placed on the radars of local, national, and federal government officials.

In 1969 and 1970, AIM developed headquarters in Milwaukee, Denver, Cleveland, and Seattle. The national organization, stationed in Minneapolis, acted as an information hub for the local sectors. Although operating under a loose leadership, each local sector operated independently to address the needs of the local urban Indigenous community.

The Trail of Broken Treaties march of 1972 was a historical milestone in the evolution of AIM. Specifically, a trail of caravans, carrying AIM and non-AIM Indigenous members traveling from Denver, Los Angeles, and Seattle, headed to Washington D.C. to present a list of grievances of Indigenous people. The goal of the caravan was to "remind elected officials of the common mistreatment and neglect of the American Indian" (Schuttler, 1991, p. 30). Twelve organizations, representing over 80 tribes, participated in the extended, yet united, ride to Washington D.C. During the trip, AIM members were to deliver a 20-point list of demands reflective of Indigenous grievances, which they believed White House Officials were accountable to address. The 20 points included "provisions concerning redress of Past grievances, resumption of treaty-making, water rights, Volition of the Bureau of Indian Affairs (BIA), and improved social, economic, and health conditions" (Schuttler, 1991, p. 30).

Prior to their arrival, caravan leaders arranged with church and religious groups in D.C. to provide lodging for Indigenous travelers. Long and behold, these same groups withdrew their invitations, and AIM members and allies, in turn, were forced to reside in rat-infested, scum motels. Thus, on November 2, 1972, more than 500 Indigenous activists took over the BIA offices building in D.C. to demand equitable lodging and swift attention to the 20 points. Louis Bruce, an Oglala from Pine Ridge, SD, Reservation and commissioner of Indian Affairs, made the following statement after visiting the building, which in turn, he later lost his job: "I'm willing to stick it out to assist you." As we make sense of police or security forces during such arrangement, it must be noted that the U.S. Army refused to let caravan members visit Arlington Cemetery for spiritual practices to honor Indigenous martyrs of war. Their rationale was "the caravan was a partisan event" (Schuttler, 1991, p. 33). As a continued practice amidst resistance by the people, the Army, or security personnel, refused to permit Indigenous people to practice their spiritual rights in a cemetery or public space. Again, police in this regard was functioning solely to protect a space of "the dead" or deceased, rather than being intentional to protect the living, or caravan Indigenous travelers, during spiritual practices. The White House, led by Richard Nixon, agreed to develop a task force to investigate the 20 points delivered by AIM members, along with $60,000 for Indigenous travelers returning home.

Due to AIM's association with the BIA office seizure in D.C., along with the 20 points, increased tension between AIM, the reservation, and more importantly, government agencies. In turn, "the FBI listed AIM members as 'key extremists'" (Schuttler, 1991, p. 34). During this same period and event, AIM transitioned its effort from urban centers to reservations, due to young populations appealing to their ideas of Indian self-determination, pride, and weariness of poverty and hardships that couple reservation life.

Several reasons may have led to the armed standoff between AIM members and FBI officials at Wounded Knee, Pine Ridge Reservation.

First, Russell Means, a primary leader of AIM, was from Pine Ridge. Second, AIM leaders visited Pine Ridge on several occasions to partake in traditional Sioux ceremonies in search of their own Indigenous heritage. Finally, in March 1972, "Raymond Yellow Thunder [was] found dead in nearby Gordon, Nebraska" (Schuttler, 1991, p. 36). According to reports, Yellow Thunder was stripped from the waist down and thrown in the center of a dance at the American Legion hall. In turn, he was found in the trunk of a car and died from internal injuries. Finally, South Dakota became known as "the Mississippi of the North" and in turn, AIM felt it necessary to focus its organizing efforts there (Schuttler, 1991, p. 36).

Early 1973 were the early stages of the escalation at Wounded Knee, as well as another police confrontation with AIM. For example, a White person was standing trial for the killing of an Indigenous man, Wesley Bad Heart Bull, in Custer, South Dakota. While AIM members traveled, met, and began negotiations inside the courthouse to increase the manslaughter charges to more serious ones, a shoving and yelling match between Bad Heart Bull's mother and an angry mob and state police ensued. "The situation escalated quickly into a riot during which the Chamber of Commerce building was burned to the ground" (Schuttler, 1991, p. 37). During this same period, Dick Wilson, elected tribal council president, was accused by some tribal members of misusing tribal funds, nepotism, and failure to hold meetings, which led to their call for his impeachment. Wilson strongly opposed AIM and represented a faction of Indigenous people who did not support AIM as well. Suggesting fear following the Custer riot, Wilson requested protection from the government, and in turn, on February 14, 1970, federal marshals from a "Special Operations Group" in Pine Ridge arrived with machine-guns and encamped at the BIA building. The Oglala Civil Rights Organization (OSCRO) was created as a response to this and they welcomed the direction, support, and leadership of AIM members. Thus, two weeks later, AIM and OSCRO seized and surrounded the village of Wounded Knee (Schuttler, 1991, p. 38). Seizing hostages, which they later did not harm, along with demanding hearings from the Senate Foreign Relations Committee (SFRC), Carter Camp, AIM leader, suggested the following surrounding the takeover: "We will occupy this town until the Government sees fit to deal with the Indian people, particularly the Oglala Sioux tribe in South Dakota." As a result, FBI and federal marshals joined forces to encircle Wounded Knee. AIM took several hostages, including representatives from religious sectors, which they were permitted to leave the compound but chose to stay in support of AIM's goals. During the standoff,

AIM submitted a four-point proposal which included an immediate evacuation of Wounded Knee by federal officers, restitution paid for personal property damage, no mass arrests, and clergy from South Dakota to observe the events. The proposal was rejected by the government. AIM received national support for their actions, which a poll indicated that 51% approved AIM's goals and 21% opposed them (Schuttler, 1991, p. 39). Nightly gunfire exchanges occurred between AIM members and federal agents, leaving two Indigenous dead and an FBI agent seriously wounded. A settlement was finally reached on May 5, which days later, the FBI agents evacuated Wounded Knee. Two trials occurred, one for non-AIM leaders and the other for AIM leaders, in which all charges levied against Indigenous people were dismissed. For the record, "none of AIM's national leadership was ever convicted for any charges arising from Wounded Knee," according to Schuttler (1991).

Two years after the court hearings, another major event occurred on Pine Ridge Reservation. On June 26, 1975, another standoff and shoot-out between FBI agents and AIM members occurred on the reservation. Two FBI agents, Jack Coler and Ronald Williams, were killed. The federal government charged and convicted AIM member Leonard Peltier for the murders. Peltier was sentenced to two consecutive life sentences and served his sentence in a federal prison. Peltier maintains his innocence of not having fired the weapon that killed the FBI agents. After spending nearly 50 years behind bars, Mr. Peltier was granted a pardon by U.S. President Joe Biden and was released from prison on February 18, 2025 (NDN Collective, 2025).

FBI Infiltration of AIM: Douglas Durham

It must be noted that covert operations facilitated by the FBI also infiltrated the ranks of AIM. Specifically, Douglas Durham, paid informant by the FBI, held esteemed positions in AIM from 1973 to 1975, including serving as public relations director, assistant director of the Des Moines, Iowa chapter, as well as national security director, director of national offices of AIM, and security for Dennis Banks. His testimony served as the primary tool to vilify, corroborate violent acts, and promote falsities about the activities of AIM during the Eastland Hearing. On March 7, 1975, AIM leaders exposed Durham as an informant (Schuttler, 1991, p. 61) and asked him to depart the group. At a press conference, he described AIM as a "legal social organization that wasn't doing anything wrong," only to later change his narrative of AIM at the Eastland Hearings as "a violent group that stated they are non-violent. They are dedicated to the overthrow of our Government, and they have trampled the civil rights of Indians and non-Indians" (Schuttler, 1991, p. 61). Despite the FBI amassing more than 316,000 file classifications on AIM, as stated, Durham's testimony was used as the sole evidence during the Eastland Hearings.

In sum, as a paid informant by the FBI, along with collecting an exponential amount of files on AIM, it becomes clear that the goal of police agents was not to support and promote the ideas, practices, and movement of AIM, but to infiltrate, repress, neutralize, and disapprove the efforts of AIM members. Brutality and arrest of occupiers, as well as killings of AIM members during standoffs, the purpose of the police remained to act as another extension of the U.S. government security apparatus, designed to maintain the subjugation and control of Indigenous and oppressed people.

Weather Underground

The Weather Underground was formed in October 1969 when a group of young White college activists who were outraged by the Vietnam War and racism in the United States united to respond to the U.S. government (i.e., military and law enforcement/policing). They were originally founded as the Weathermen, but later changed the name of the group to the Weather Underground. Before organizing as the Weathermen, they were originally members of the *Students for a Democratic Society* (SDS) group in New York, Chicago, and other cities in the United States; however, they left the organization because they disagreed with SDS's peaceful protests in response to the Vietnam War and police brutality of Black folks (Lambert, 2024). They believed armed resistance was the necessary response to the U.S. involvement in the Vietnam War, police brutality, and racism in the United States. They organized and committed numerous acts of violent resistance against the government, specifically using explosive devices in government buildings (i.e., capital, pentagon, etc.) in response to the violent terror of the Vietnam War, police brutality, and racism. According to the 2022 podcast *Mother Country Radicals*, these explosive devices targeted property, not people (Dohrn, 2022).

There are, however, some critiques of the Weather Underground group and movement. For example, in Chicago in 1969, the Weather Underground organized the "kick-ass" brawl, a four-day protest against the Vietnam War that resulted in the destruction of property and serious injuries for both protestors of the Weather Underground and Chicago police. One of the critics of these demonstrations was Chairman Fred Hampton (*former Minister of Information of the Black Panther Party, Chicago, Illinois*) who in an interview described the Weathermen as "opportunistic, adventuristic, and Custeristic," and that confrontations with police were "revolutionary child's play." Chairman Fred stated that the Weathermen were "leading people into a confrontation they are not prepared for" (Workers of the World,

2020). Additionally, Chairman Fred argued that some of the Weather Underground's actions represented suicidal violence that places people at risk of being hurt; reckless, violent actions endanger people; and extreme violence brings even more violence from the purveyors of imperialist violence, the U.S. government (Workers of the World, 2020).

In response to some of the critiques, it is important to note that the extreme focus on the acts and demonstrations of violence orchestrated by the Weather Underground seems to ignore or distract attention from the acts of [state] violence committed by the U.S. government and its agents. Additionally, leaders of the Weather Underground maintain that no person was ever physically hurt – they only destroyed property. Finally, after more than a decade of living underground, leaders and members began to resurface and turn themselves in for the crimes they were accused and charged with committing. However, many of them were not imprisoned because of the unethical and illegal behavior (i.e., illegal wiretaps and other forms of surveillance) of the U.S. government, namely the FBI, while pursuing them. Thus, the government frequently dismissed cases against leaders and members of the Weather Underground rather than allow the public to know that the government acted illegally.

Militarization of Policing

Although most citizens understand police as domestic keepers of safety, the reality of their unchecked power, when combined with armament and weaponry, tends to counter such beliefs and arguments. The police can and should be understood as the gatekeepers of social control of the populus, purveyors of violence to repress social resistance and uprisings, along with protectors of assets and properties of economic elites and capitalists. It is through these understandings that we find clarity surrounding the purpose of policing, as well as "why" the police militarization becomes necessary. Thus, the police, in its totality, can be understood as the domestic military wing of the State that maintains social control of the populus, while protecting the interest of the ruling elite, or those who control the economic production and distribution in the United States. Three factors of militarizing police must be considered: police budget, weapons and armament, and their ability to act as judge and jury in a supposed criminal situation.

Police Budget

It is no coincidence that the police budget remains the highest among social services in most major cities in the United States. The budget of law enforcement, or "public safety," usually supersedes those for all social services, including mental, physical, educational, and recreational services. Police salaries, paid time off (PTO or vacation), as well as paid overtime, constitute the bulk of police pay and increases. One article reported that some law enforcement officers, including those in schools (10.8% higher than some HS teachers), can earn well over six-figure salaries, which in a school setting, they would earn one of the highest salaries below the principals (UTEP Connect, 2023; USA Facts Team, 2025). Furthermore, we must recognize that police budgets are always utilized to pay attorney fees, court appearances, and legal settlements related to police misconduct, brutality, or officer-involved shootings and homicides. Finally, through the ongoing campaigning by police unions for "more funding" and media propaganda surrounding the need for more police, police departments in some major cities, such as Chicago, New York City, and Los Angeles, have larger budgets than the military of several developed countries around the globe. For instance, according to the U.S. Census Bureau, in 2022, police budgets, nationwide, were covered by state and local government funds and grant programs, which accounted for $140 billion. Moreover, local governments in particular funded $119 billion for police, close to 85% of the total budget, respectively (USA Facts Team, 2025). Scholars further note how, since the late 1990s, the U.S. Department of Defense has funneled more than $7.2 billion in military armament to law enforcement agencies (James, 2024).

Military Weapons and Armament

The militarization of police over the past several decades has remained a continuous and consistent phenomenon. Since the early 1980s, following the inception of the "War on Drugs" and "War on Crime" campaigns against poor Black and Brown communities, the U.S. government has continued to increase the weapons and armament of police, along with their ability to "combat crime" and maintain social control in poor and low-income settings. As a result, war becomes a domestic or national phenomenon waged by police, which in turn, the lines of policing and combating insurgents are blurred.

For example, Peter Kraska (2007), in his seminal work titled *Militarization and Policing*, provides important insights and evidence to help readers better understand the blurred line between policing and militarism in the United States. Specifically, he defines *militarism* "as a set of beliefs, values, and assumptions that stress the use of force and threat of violence as the most appropriate and efficacious means to solve problems" through the utility of "military power, hardware, organization, operations, and technology" (p. 3). He further suggests that *Militarization* can be understood as "the implementation of the ideology, militarism . . . the process of arming, organizing, planning, training for, threatening, and sometimes implementing violent conflict" (p. 3). Thus, ***police militarization*** "is simply the process whereby civilian police increasingly draw from, and pattern themselves around, the tenets of militarism and the military model" (Kraska, 2007, p. 3).

Kraska (2007) provides four tangible indicators of police militarization, which include: material, cultural, organizational, and operational. By using these four indicators, he argues that a primary aim for readers is to understand the "degree and extent" to which civilian police forces are militarized, or granted the "state sanctioned capacity to use physical force to accomplish their respective objectives" (p. 3). In an attempt to understand the role of the military model on contemporary policing, the author conducted a two-year-long ethnography of multi-jurisdictional *Special Weapons and Tactics (SWAT)* teams. He spent hundreds of hours training and going on actual deployment with SWAT teams as tools for data collection. The author provides important information surrounding *police paramilitary units' (PPUs)* and SWAT teams' behaviors and culture.

For instance, he suggests that PPUs model their appearance, tactics, operations, weaponry, and culture from special operations units of the military, such as Navy Seals. Similar to the military, PPUs possess heavy weaponry, are trained for hostage rescue, and operate some of the latest and advanced technology. Overall, most small and major cities with 25 to 50,000 citizenry possess a PPU, with an exponential growth rate for small cities (25,000 or less) since the 1980s from 20% to 80% (Kraska, 2007, p. 6). When considering PPU deployment for majority of drug raids (80%), Kraska (2007) stated,

> There has been more than a 1,400% increase in the total number of police paramilitary (PPU) deployments, or callouts, between 1980 and 2000. Today, an estimated 45,000 SWAT-team deployments are conducted yearly among those departments surveyed; in the early 1980s there was an average of about 3,000 (Kraska, 2007). The trend-line demonstrated that this growth began during the drug war of the late 1980s and early 1990s.
>
> *(p. 6)*

He further provided evidence of the militarization of domestic police based on data from no knock/quick knock SWAT raids. According to Kraska (2007), these raids "constitute a proactive contraband raid" in which their primary aim is "to collect evidence (usually, drugs, guns, and/or money) from inside a private residence . . . essentially a crude form of drug investigation" (p. 7). As most may be aware, no-knock/quick knock SWAT raids typically involve predawn, unbeknownst searches by armed police in military gear. At times, they may use battering rams to enter the house, flash grenades pre entry, and all residents are expected to comply with their demands. Civilians, in turn, may be severely injured and lethally killed during SWAT raids. Kraska (2007) recorded more than 275 instances of seriously botched SWAT raids on private residences (p. 7). He reminds us that botched raids often destroy communities and often lead to the disbandment of SWAT departments (Balko, 2006; Kraska, 2007, p. 7). Finally, he notes that SWAT raids and their utility are not forced mandates by the government to local and domestic police; however, "they are the result of police departments choosing to use an extreme and highly dangerous tactic . . . for small-time drug possessors and dealers" (Kraska, 2007, p. 8).

Police Unions

History

Some scholars would argue that the major reason police are not accountable for acts of terrorism, brutality, and violence against U.S. residents is a result of police unions. The formation of police unions originated in 1919 in Boston, MA. Specifically, the main purpose of police unions in its origin was to improve the work conditions, hours worked, and wages of officers. However, the capitalist ruling elite of Boston and critics were fearful of police officers going on strike due to a union. As a result, in "September 1919, 1,147 Boston police officers went on strike after 19 officers were suspended for violating an anti-union policy" (Halvorson, 2022, p. 4). The strike failed, with all officers being fired and not reinstated, and in turn, no-strike clauses and policies were developed to prevent future strikes by police, and any working-class people who wanted to seize power from the hands of the capitalist ruling elite.

The next, and successful, attempts of police unionization evolved during the Civil Rights and Black Power Struggle during the 1960s. Criticism of police brutality and terrorism by activists and organizers was rampant during this period, essentially leading to the creation and establishment of police unions. While these grassroots groups were calling for internal police investigations and pressure to put an end to police misconduct, killings, and abuse, police departments counteracted these calls with pushback against police reforms, and in turn, moved for the establishment of a police union. It must be noted that the *Law Enforcement Officers' Bill of Rights (LEOBORs)* was established alongside police unions during the late 1960s and early 1970s (Halvorson, 2022, pp. 4–5).

Law Enforcement Officers' Bill of Rights (LEOBORs)

What is a LEOBOR? A LEOBOR is a constitution that provides protections (from investigation and prosecution), primarily at the local and state levels, to law enforcement officers accused of engaging in acts of misconduct (Halvorson, 2022, p. 5). When considering the impact of a LEOBOR and civilians' ability to hold police accountable for terrorizing or abusing citizens, the following protections of police must be noted:

> These protections include delays before interviewing officers accused of misconduct, access to all (or most) of the evidence that might be presented against them before being interrogated, restricted public access to complaint data, prohibitions on anonymous complaints, and limits on the ability of people outside of a police department (such as civilian review boards) to investigate misconduct complaints filed by civilians.
>
> *(Place, 2018; Halvorson, 2022, p. 5)*

In 1974, the first LEOBOR was developed in Florida and Maryland, and according to the *Police Accountability Project (2021)*, at least 23 states currently have a "codified" LEOBOR that protects officers facing accusations of abuse and misconduct. It is further relevant to highlight that LEOBORs most often exist in States and cities with large urban populations (i.e., California, Pennsylvania, and Illinois) and may not exist in States and cities without this arrangement (i.e., North Dakota, Vermont, and Wyoming – Halvorson, 2022, p. 6). In addition, in 1974, many Civil Rights and Freedom Struggle organizations had been dismantled, neutralized by secret service and State-sanctioned operations, and many members killed by police, special agents, and secret government organizations (i.e., Counter Intelligence Program or COINTELPRO – Bukhari, 2010; Enck-Wanzer, 2010; Muntaqim, 2020; Schuttler, 1991). Thus, the passing of the first LEOBOR seemed timely to protect the police as a local and state security apparatus, for the State, amidst the ongoing neutralization and assassination of key members of the civil rights and liberation struggles by government-sanctioned personnel in the United States (*Note: On December 4, 1969, Chairman Fred Hampton, Minister of Defense for the BPP, Chicago, IL, was killed by FBI and Chicago PD during a 4:00 AM shoot-in and warrantless house raid, which he was shot in the head at point blank range while asleep in bed. Hampton was sedated by spiked kool-aid planted by FBI Informant, William O'neal* – Abu-Jamal, 2016, pp. 150–153).

In its origin, as appears to be the case today, LEOBORs are fought for by police unions to thwart police accountability by offering them special privileges from being prosecuted by the courts (Rushin, 2015). Furthermore, police unions are used for political lobbying and donating funds to political candidates that are pro-police unions and unwilling to challenge them. Statutes or policies developed and supported by police unions are often used to keep investigations of police "Internal" (in other words, police investigating themselves), which eliminates nonpolice citizenry from holding them accountable (Bies, 2017; Place, 2018; Rushin, 2015). It becomes clear as to *why*, following a police-involved homicide, no outside entities are permitted to 1) investigate the crime scene, 2) immediately interview the officer involved, and/or 3) hold future court to determine the innocence or guilt of the officer's actions leading to a person's death.

Contract Provisions and Civilian Review Boards (CRBs)

Another important element of the challenge to hold police accountable for acts of abuse and homicide is due to police contract provisions. These provisions do not support, but actively work against improving police accountability. For example, some scholars have argued that such provisions create an "alternative justice system" (Fisk & Richardson, 2017; McKesson, Sinyangwe, Elzie, & Packnett, 2016) which protects police from facing accusations of crime and abuse as would be the case for a community resident. These six major contract provisions include the following:

> Early disqualification of misconduct complaints, delaying interrogations of officers accused of misconduct, giving officers access to additional information before an interrogation (in comparison to criminal suspects who are not sworn officers), limiting disciplinary consequences for officers accused of misconduct, city governments paying legal fees of officers involved in instances of alleged misconduct, and preventing the retainment of an officer's disciplinary history.
>
> *(Halvorson, 2022, p. 12)*

In addition, it is necessary to remain critical of civilian review boards (CRBs), despite their intention and attempts to have oversight of police misconduct, abuse, and killing of citizens. For example, despite the police union's resistance to CRBs, there are major issues about this structure that must be noted. For instance, "civilian review boards have been historically ineffective, because they have had little to no discretionary power to impose punishments against police officers found guilty of misconduct" (Halvorson, 2022, p. 19; Simonson, 2021). This remains the case for most, if not all, CRBs in the United States. As noted by some authors, CRBs, in their current arrangement, only act as a structure to review civilian complaints and accusations against police, and in turn, make recommendations "to police managers on what they believe would be an appropriate consequence" (p. 19). Thus, the power to determine or execute appropriate actions to hold police accountable remains in the hands of police leadership (i.e., chief of police, at times city mayor) or city/county executives (Bobb, 2003; Fegley, 2020; Halvorson, 2022, p. 19).

On a final note, an important reminder to highlight regarding police unions and provisional contracts is that cities, or working-class tax dollars, cover the costs related to police misconduct. For example, McKesson, Sinyangwe, Elzie, and Packnett (2016) remind us that police union contracts commonly *require* that cities cover the financial costs handed down by the judicial system against an officer. These costs may include, but not limited to, legal fees, financial settlements, continued salary, as well as restitution pay to the officer under investigation. Such clauses were present in 49% of union contracts studied (Halvorson, 2022, p. 20; McKesson et al., 2016). A prime example of these "outcomes" was that in 2022, New York City paid $135 million in settlements stemming from 971 lawsuits and paid more than $500 million in police misconduct settlements over a six-year period (Meko, 2024). Thus, the financial burden surrounding police terrorism, abuse, and misconduct is covered by the hard-earned tax dollars of working-class people in the United States. Such a financial arrangement between potential purveyors of violence and their victims is not based on the decision of working-class people, but primarily due to contracts, provisions, and unionization of police. Thus, local and national policy and "paperwork" are major protectors and enablers of police terrorism and abuse.

In sum, it is important to understand how historically, it was not solely due to people's fear to resist, struggle, and fight against police terrorism that maintained this phenomenon in the United States. Nor was it solely due to people's inability to organize, mobilize, and collectivize solutions to abolish policing and/or gain community control of public safety, at the local, state, and national levels. The evidence is quite the opposite: Citizens who accuse police of misconduct, abuse, or the extreme, homicide of an individual, are thwarted from holding police accountable due to policies, provisional contracts, political lobbying (e.g., bribery), and internal investigations only (e.g., Systemic factors, or Violence), in the aftermath of such occurrences. Thus, we can conclude that the problem is not our unwillingness to struggle against this detriment of human society (*the evidence speaks to the contrary*), but primarily due to a system that protects and privileges the local, state, and national security apparatus (police and police unions) from any misdeeds, wrongdoing, and more importantly, crimes committed. This line of inquiry is worth further study and investigation for individuals interested and willing to dismantle policing in its current form, while simultaneously transferring governing power to community members to control, investigate, and expend consequences for police harm, brutality, and killing of a resident, when necessary.

Part II: Contemporary

Police Killings of U.S. Citizens

As some readers may be aware, the United States of America (U.S.A.) has held the number one position among developed countries in regard to police killings of its citizenry. Several online databases, including *KilledBy-Police.net, the Washington Post,* and *Mapping Police Violence*, have made valiant attempts to tally the frequency of U.S. civilians killed by police over the last decade. For example, the United States ranks #7 among the top countries with the highest numbers of police killings in the world (Philippines (6,069+), Brazil (5,804), and Venezuela (5,287) among the top three), in which the United States is the only developed country on the top ten list (WPR, 2023). Developed countries can be understood as a sovereign state possessing a mature economy, technologically advanced infrastructure, and can also include a country's GDP per capita, literacy rate, life expectancy, political stability, and access to electricity. Furthermore, between 2013 and 2016, 4,289 citizens were killed by police and law enforcement agents in the United States, an average of 1,072 lives per year (Mapping Police Violence, 2024). Moreover, sources indicate that the U.S. police have killed nearly 1,000 people yearly since 2015 (Mapping Police Violence, 2024).

In addition, 8 of the 100 largest police departments in the United States – *Reno, NV; Oklahoma City, OK; Santa Ana, CA; Anaheim, CA; St. Louis, MO; Scottsdale, AZ; Hialeah, FL; and Madison, WI* – kill Black men at higher rates than the U.S. murder rate (WPR, 2023). Furthermore, despite Blacks or African Americans making up 13% of the total U.S. population, they constituted 24% of all police killings between 2015 and 2019. Finally, there were 20 and 17 days in 2016 and 2017, respectively, when the police did not kill an individual in the United States. In these two years, a total of 1,070 and 1,098 people were killed by police in 2016 and 2017, respectively (Mapping Police Violence, 2024). A major social, political, and physical health challenge surrounding police killings in the United States is the fact that most police kill individuals with impunity, which these acts are typically *JUSTIFIED* by the courts as legal grounds for police use of lethal force. It is an unsafe position to assume that police operate and work in the same capacity as other social service providers who are paid by working-class tax dollars (Rodriquez, 2023, p. 127). The police, in its historical and contemporary sense, is the only social force that can and will kill citizenry with impunity, and in turn, their acts of violence toward us are sanctioned and treated as *JUSTIFIED* practices by the courts and those that govern them.

Police Killings of Youth in the United States (2016/2017)

Police killings of youth, including children and teens, remain a social and public epidemic in the United States. For example, at first glance and review of victims killed by police in the United States derived from Mapping Police Violence database (Mapping Police Violence, 2024), we clearly see that teens, whether they are 16, 17, or 19, are killed by police. What remains unfortunate is that those youth younger than 16 may not be counted among the victims of police killings (Staggers-Hakim, 2016; Strohlic, 2014). Some researchers say it may be due to respect for age and/or simply overlooking these youth victims of police violence. Yet, the facts remain that children and teens have been killed by or lost their lives at the hands of police, with impunity. In other words, despite the 116 youth who were killed by police between January 2016 and August 2017, most of these acts were *JUSTIFIED*, or state-sanctioned with impunity. In other words, it is not just adults who are killed by police and the act justified by the courts, but also youth. Their families and loved ones are left to endure the ongoing pain and suffering from their violent and traumatic deaths, while bearing the reactions by cops, which oftentimes can include harassment, intimidation, and lack of empathy (Outland et al., 2020).

Impact of Youth Killed by Police on Survivors

Traumatic Grief Following Violent Deaths

Trauma grief can be defined as a clinical diagnosis of persistent complex grief (PCG)/prolonged grief disorder (PGD) with comorbid characteristics of Post-Traumatic Stress Disorder (PTSD) and Major Depressive Disorder (MDD) (Smid et al., 2015). Past scholars have uprooted the relationship between peoples' experiences of PGD, PTSD, and Depression following violent deaths (Boelen et al., 2015; Denderen et al., 2017; Kaltman & Bonanno, 2001; Nickerson et al., 2014; Saindon et al., 2014). Furthermore, social scientists have taken note of PG in the aftermath of the violent death of children. For example, Djelantik and Colleagues (2017) explored symptoms of PGD, PTSD, and depression following violent deaths in a Dutch community sample. Using a latent class analysis of PGD, PTSD, and depression, researchers discovered that violent causes of death, primarily related to losing a child, were associated with PGD along with combined PGD/PTSD class membership. This finding is indicative of past research on complicated bereavement in the aftermath of violent death, in which violent causes were related to heightened experiences of distress among participants (Boelen et al., 2015; Nickerson et al., 2014).

Furthermore, research discovered a link between cognitive challenges and individuals' experiencing traumatic grief following a violent death. For example, Baddeley and Colleagues (2015) explored the association between death imagery and PTSD, depression, and/or CGD symptoms in 130 treatment-seeking homicide survivors who were on average, 3.5 years post loss. They discovered that death images and thoughts were positively associated with depression, PTSD, and CGD symptoms. In addition, homicide survivors were more likely to report thoughts of revenge compared to survivors of suicide. Heeke and Colleagues (2017) further acknowledged the correlation between PGD and ruminating thoughts of the homicidally bereft. Moreover, Boelen and Colleagues (2015) denoted cognitive-behavioral variables mediating the impact of violent loss, in which people bereaved by violent loss had significantly higher symptoms of PGD, PTSD, and depression than those bereaved by nonviolent loss.

Nakajima and Colleagues (2012) further investigated the prevalence of complicated grief (CG) for bereaved families experiencing natural versus violent death of a loved one. They suggest that bereaved families caused by violent death of a member were more likely to struggle with CG symptoms than those who experienced the natural loss of a loved one (e.g., terminal illness). The researchers further state, Violent death is not only unexpected, but is caused by violence, and in turn, the bereaved family experience of violent death is significantly different than a natural death. Violent death made "sense-making" difficult (Nakajima et al., 2012). Sense-making can be understood as an intermediate factor for helping a bereaved family to accept death as a natural part of life, or as a major contributor to the severity of CG (Nakajima et al., 2012).

In addition, social scientists discovered mixed results about an individual's ability to make sense of the violent death of a loved one. On the one hand, Lichtenthal and Colleagues (2010) discovered that no individuals were able to make sense during the bereavement stage of their loved one's traumatic death. On the other hand, Bogensperger and Lueger-Schuster's (2014) study discovered more than 80% of participants identified at least one reason to find meaning in the violent death of a family member. Thus, these mixed findings further validate the urgency to understand the impact of youth killed by police on the psychological, social, and emotional well-being of family members and survivors.

Finally, Stiles (2020) investigated the long-term impact of bereavement and grief of highly publicized violent deaths on survivors. Specifically, due to survivors' experiences of continued public scrutiny from media outlets (i.e.,

TV and social media), she noted that highly publicized violent deaths can have a profound impact on survivors' cognitive functioning. The researcher further discovered a high probability for survivors to experience heightened distress and anxiety as a result of ongoing court cases and trials coupled with the uncertainty of receiving justice for their deceased family member (Stiles, 2020). In addition, Nakajima and Colleagues (2012) further validate these outcomes. They noted that bereaved families of violent deaths, oftentimes, can be slandered, discriminated against, and portrayed negatively by the media and community members, along with stress and anxiety related to public interviews, court appearances, and probable outcomes of the case. Thus, these experiences can have a direct impact on the family's grieving and bereavement process, and at times, may result in social distrust and isolation and trigger PTSD symptoms, "making it difficult for the bereaved to seek support" (Nakajima et al., 2012, pp. 211–212).

Youth Social and Emotional Challenges Following Violent Death

Research investigated the impact of violent deaths on youth's mental and emotional well-being. Specifically, Rheingold and her Colleagues (2012) explored the prevalence and mental health responses of a national sample of 3,614 adolescent (ages 12 to 17) homicide survivors in the United States. Using structured telephone interviews as a primary method for data collection, the results denoted that 1 in 5 (20%) adolescents reported homicides of family or friends. In addition, youth survivors of homicide were significantly more likely to report struggles with depression, PTSD symptoms, and substance abuse. Finally, African Americans and Hispanics were overrepresented among teen homicide survivors (Rheingold et al., 2012). Although these findings shed light on the interconnectedness between homicide and youth survivors' mental health challenges, they do not highlight young people's responses when a child or teen loved one is killed by police. Thus, further research is necessary in order to understand the impact of youth killed by police on survivors, primarily other youth.

In addition, research suggests that police killings can have an adverse influence on the emotional and social well-being of teenagers. For example, Staggers-Hakim (2016) conducted a study with 16 African American adolescent males, 14–18 years old, regarding the impact of national police killings of Black teens on their mental and social development. Using focus groups as a primary method for data collection, findings revealed that according to fear responses of the young men, police killings, in general, traumatized most participants. Moreover, young men who were removed from community violence were especially traumatized following exposure to young Black males' deadly encounters with police (Staggers-Hakim, 2016). The author also noted that although discussions among the youth were difficult at times, several young men acknowledged and described participating and discussing national police killings with peers as being a "cathartic experience" (Staggers-Hakim, 2016, p. 397).

In sum, the abovementioned findings are valuable in understanding the experiences of homicide and violent death survivors, in general. However, limited research has been conducted to understand the experiences of survivors, especially the family and loved ones, in the aftermath of a youth killed by police. In order for service providers to adequately support these survivors, it is necessary to understand their experiences in the aftermath of these occurrences. In other words, their narratives or stories about the impact of police killings on their daily lives may provide important information regarding necessary solutions and support services for survivors of youth killed by police.

Treatment and Interventions Following Violent Death

Several interventions to address the complex mental and emotional challenges of violent death survivors have shown promise in recent times. For example, Restorative Retelling (RR) has proven to be a useful, brief-structured group intervention for this population. Saindon and Colleagues (2014) used RR as a psychotherapy intervention to assist 51 violent loss survivors who were at risk for developing PTSD, depression, and PGD. The authors found that RR had a significant impact on reducing participants' bereavement symptoms of depression, avoidance, and PGD over time. Moreover, the ten weekly sessions were well tolerated by participants, being that the majority of individuals completed the program (Saindon et al., 2014). Furthermore, Rheingold et al. (2015) conducted an RR group intervention with 91 violent death survivors. The authors examined the effectiveness of RR on symptoms of trauma grief as well as closeness in relationship of participants to the deceased. Participants completed PTSD, PGD, and depression measures at pre- and post assessment, as well as one-year follow-up (Rheingold et al., 2015). They noted significant reductions in survivors' PTSD and Depression symptoms post assessment, as well as reduction in all three domains at one-year follow-up. In sum, RR group intervention can be beneficial in reducing trauma grief symptoms of survivors of violent death.

Finally, researchers have proposed integrated and module-based interventions for survivors of violent death. Specifically, Smid and Colleagues (2015) proposed an integrated intervention that used *Brief Eclectic Psychotherapy for Traumatic Grief* (BEP-TG). This 16-week group consists of five effective elements designed to treat symptoms of traumatic grief: 1) Information and motivation, 2) grief-focused exposure, 3) memorabilia and writing assignments, 4) finding meaning and activation, and 5) a farewell ritual. The authors note that BEP-TG holds promise to reduce traumatic grief symptoms of violent death survivors, due to the emphasis on meaning-making assignments and opportunities for members to develop their trauma narrative (Smid et al., 2015). Furthermore, Rheingold and Williams (2018) proposed a module-based intervention to address complex mental health demands of violent loss survivors. *Grief Recovery with an Individualized Evidence-Based Formulation approach (GRIEF)* model is designed to target three symptoms of trauma grief: PTSD, PGD, and depression. According to case examples of participants' experiences of the 12–20 week sessions, the authors noted significant reductions in all three domains of participants' traumatic grief. The authors make mention of an existing gap in treating the complex needs of violent death survivors and recommend the use of flexible and empirical-based treatment to address their mental and emotional challenges (Rheingold & Williams, 2018).

In sum, several interventions to address symptoms related to traumatic grief can benefit the family and loved ones of homicide survivors. Moreover, these interventions can also be useful to address complex trauma and grief of the family and friends of youth killed by police. However, two factors related to this population's traumatic grief must be noted. First, some families and loved ones of youth killed by police may lack access to treatment and interventions in their local communities (Huang, 2018). In addition, due to their experiences of scrutiny in the media surrounding the death of their loved one by police, these individuals may be hesitant to seek out services based on their lack of trust in authority figures (Stiles, 2020). As a result, service providers who work with survivors of youth killed by police must consider the necessity of visiting the community of these individuals, to 1) identify their mental, social, emotional, and financial needs and to 2) determine appropriate culturally sensitive remedies to address them.

Impact of Colonial and State-Sanctioned Violence on Survivors

In Frantz Fanon's (2004) seminal work, *The Wretched of the Earth*, he describes in detail the impact of the Colonial War, or Colonialism, on colonized subjects or an oppressed people. He reminds us that the colonized "will be bandaging the countless and sometimes indelible wounds inflicted on our people by the colonialist onslaught" (p. 181). He goes on to suggest that "Imperialism. . .sows seeds of decay here and there that must be mercilessly rooted out from our land and from our minds" (p. 181). Dr. Fanon states that "colonization, in its very essence, already appeared to be a great purveyor of psychiatric hospitals . . . since 1954" as psychiatrists attempted to change the colonized subject to fit "into a social environment of the colonial type" (Fanon, 2004, pp. 181–182). Due to the systematized negation of the other, a constant denial of the other of any aspect of "humanity," Dr. Fanon (2004) suggests that colonialism forces the colonized to constantly ask the question: "Who am I in reality?" (p. 182). He denotes that this defensive position born of violence between the colonized and colonizer reveals the colonized personality, in which our understanding of this sensibility is clarified through study and appreciation of the scope and depths of wounds inflicted on colonized subjects (Fanon, 2004, p. 182). In other words, a close analysis regarding the impact of colonialism or its remnants on oppressed people is warranted. Furthermore, a clarifying revelation is Fanon's (2004) suggestion that throughout history, the colonized subject has remained a "human being" under colonial regimes and institutions. Thus, this socialization can be understood as the practice by the colonized subject, or oppressed person, to fit the mold or appropriate a social identity of humanness in a colonial situation. Finally, he suggests that when colonization remains unchallenged by armed resistance, when the sum of harmful stimulants exceeds a certain threshold, the colonized defenses collapse, and many of them end up in psychiatric institutions. Thus, according to Fanon (2004), the act of the colonized to "not" struggle in an armed war for liberation from the colonizer is a breeding ground for mental disorders (Fanon, 2004, pp. 182–183).

This literature review concludes with discourse related to the impact of colonial wars and state-sanctioned violence (i.e., police terrorism) on the mental, social, and emotional outcomes of survivors, primarily freedom fighters and their families.

We first begin with the impact of colonialism on the Indigenous people of Turtle Island. As many are aware, when the first colonizers arrived at Turtle Island with Colombo and his pirates, Turtle Island was a beautiful geography, plentiful of raw materials and natural resources, along with a population who strived to exist as one with Nature and the Earth. However, to ensure a fair discourse on the matter, we must be reminded that the Indigenous people were the first to experience 1) Genocide and 2) institutional slavery on Turtle Island. Gord Hill (2010) reminds us of the countless Indigenous people who were killed by colonial forces, as well as the raw materials and resources that were plundered during the European colonization process. Each voyage carried a specific mission: To continue the exploitation of Indigenous people and their land. We are further reminded of the Colonial Boarding Schools that forcefully kidnapped, contained, and imposed European beliefs, values, and doctrines on Indigenous youth. The countless gravesites discovered in recent times at the territory of these boarding schools in Canada are examples of such atrocities (Dog & Erdoes, 1991). Finally, although historically existing under a government of matriarchy and socialist principles of *from one to all* (communal ways of existing), the Indigenous people of Turtle Island were forced to give up their land, relocate to small locales of the reservation (i.e., concentration camps), only to become detached from Nature, the Ecology, and their Language and Culture, which their ancestors respected and adhered, along with being taxed for work and their land by the colonizers who forcefully stole Turtle Island (Redvers et al., 2023).

These atrocities over time have contributed to the mental, emotional, and social challenges that exist among Indigenous people. For instance, some scholars report depression, anxiety, PTSD, and alcoholism among the mental and social challenges navigated by Indigenous families. Colonial land theft, displacement, and separation from the Ecology are major contributors to these challenges. Furthermore, poverty, health care, and getting one's basic needs met, along with domestic abuse and suicide, have also been identified as issues facing Indigenous people due to being forced by government to exist on reservations that are at-risk/sensitive to the detriments of climate change (Redvers et al., 2023). If Fanon's (2004) notion to the high probability of mental disorders during colonial wars is true, then it seems misguided to place blame solely on Indigenous people for their contemporary challenges, but to place this burden on the shoulders of the *Purveyors of Colonialism* and those who have maintained these historically violent practices on Turtle Island. Thus, in order to understand, support, struggle with, and sincerely Love Indigenous people, it is necessary that we reckon with their experiences of historic and contemporary colonialism and institutionalized violence, respectively, which in turn have displaced a people of the Earth from their culture, land, language, and ancestral heritage.

It is further necessary to make sense of the economic, mental, and social challenges that have historically confronted Black people or Africans in the United States. First, we must never forget the dark legacy of European colonialism that plagued Africans in the United States, historically and presently. For example, we must never forget that during the European colonial conquest, Africans were kidnapped in mass from their homeland, enchained, and faced the colonizer's barrel of the gun, where they died, fought, and died again, to resist the Transatlantic Passage that led to the evolution of Africans as chattel property to Europeans in the Western world (Abu-Jamal, 2016). John Henry Clark reminds us that Africans did not arrive at the borders of Turtle Island as "slaves," but as Africans (IBWL21.org, 2024). Thus, when kidnapped Africans were placed on public auction blocks by the colonizers and their lackeys, auctioned to the highest bidder, and in turn, sold as objects, it was at this moment when the political, cultural, and social context turned the African into a slave of Europeans in the United States. unchecked barbary and sadism practiced by slaveholders, including rape, mass breeding, brutal beatings and torture, along with public killings of rebellious slaves, were normative practices on the plantation (Rodney, 1982). To supposedly end the violent institution of chattel slavery, only to replace this institution and place in bondage the stolen African into sharecropping, Jim Crow and legal lynching Era of the United States remained the continued experiences of most Blacks (Wright et al., 2022; Blackman, 2008). Europeans in the United States reveled in the practice of legalized lynching of Blacks, which included public parades, family gatherings and picnics, auctioning body parts of the deceased, and celebratory gestures and smiles of individuals dressed in all White (Roberts, 1997; DeGruy, 2005). Indeed, legal lynching of Blacks was far from random occurrences, but according to media propaganda, was a natural part of the social and cultural fabrics of European Americans (Hess, 2000; Wells, 1970/2020).

The colonial wars against Africans further extended to the 1900s. From the organized disruption, neutralization, and alienation of W.E.B. DuBois and Marcus Garvey and the NIAO in the early 1900s (Burden-Stelly, 2023), the continued repression and killings of Black leaders during the Civil Rights and Mississippi Freedom Movement in the 1960/1970s (Umoja, 2013), to the repression and neutralization of the Black Power Movement, including SNIC (Whitaker, 2023), the Black Panthers (Abu-Jamal, 2016), and BLA during the 1960–1980s (Bukhari, 2010; Muntaqim, 2020), it must be understood that this legacy of government disruption of "Black Progress" has a grave impact on the mental and social challenges endured by Blacks in the United States during contemporary times.

A prime example is a consideration of contemporary Gang Violence (Bloods & Crips) in relation to the History of Armed Resistance in the Black Community. *Bastards of the Party* (Sloan, 2005), a documentary that chronicled the evolution of gangs in the Aftermath of the Black Power Movement, provides important discourse and demonstrations of this connection. The moderator was interested in understanding the transition of Black grassroots organizations from helping and protecting the community to becoming local enemies, which can include intercommunal violence, domestic disputes, fratricide, and homicide, to street gangs or tribes (Williams, 2007). He suggests that this transition was primarily based on government intervention and ushering in nonprofit institutions instead of revolutionary programs to transform and evolve the community. Furthermore, the government's "War on Drugs" in the 1980s further exacerbated intercommunal gang violence, which he denoted that members were able to purchase and distribute large quantities of crack cocaine and other drugs, while increasing their armament and weaponry to protect their interest and territory. Countless gang members were killed by one another or the police, while others were thrown in prison for extensive sentences (*Catch 22, see*

Outland, Symbolic Meaning of Violence, 2019), thus, influencing the evolution of Mass Incarceration and the Prison Industrial Complex in the United States for drug offenses (Alexander, 2012) and state-sanctioned counterinsurgency and terror of inmates in state and federal prisons (Burton, 2023). In his seminal work, Tip of the Spear, Orisami Burton (2023) defines Counterinsurgency imposed on incarcerated individuals by the carceral system:

> Counterinsurgency, according to the U.S. Army, is a style of warfare that involves military, paramilitary, political, economic, psychological, and civic actions taken by a government to defeat insurgency . . . the planners and administrators of this carceral siege aim to crush the Revolt by deploying a range of techniques, both "hard" and "soft" across these terrains.
>
> *(p. 4)*

Thus, we are encouraged to learn about the impact of these continued forms of institutionalized violence on Blacks in the United States. As stated with Indigenous people, Blacks must be understood according to our experiences of Colonialism and Institutionalized Violence in the United States. Reminded by Fanon (2004), the colonial war is bound to create a multitude of mental health disorders, in turn, filling the psychiatric facilities with colonized subjects. Thus, as long as Blacks in the United States have to endure, struggle, and navigate institutionalized violence, then we can expect a continuation of some of the economic, mental, and social challenges among Black people. For instance, the infiltration of the Central Intelligence Agency (CIA) and other government personnel of the BPP led to acts of fratricide by its members. Fratricide can be defined as the killing of one's brother, sister, or fellow comrade. Indeed, although government agents and informants of these organizations orchestrated such acts of fratricide, at times, Black Panther loyal members were still participants in these atrocities (Abu-Jamal, 2016). Acts of fratricide have also been contested to have occurred in the Nation of Islam (NOI) surrounding the assassination of Malcolm X or El-Hajj Malik Shabazz (Goldman, 1979; Kondo, 1993). Thus, the mental, emotional, and social remnants of fratricide cannot be easily dismissed in our contemporary times. Historical fratricide of an organization can lead to distrust, fear, political paranoia, substance abuse and addiction, etc. of contemporary members or elder freedom fighters. Moreover, the capture, torture, and extensive *death sentences* in prison of Black Freedom Fighters, Black Liberation Army, and Black Panther Veterans (Kamau Sadiki, Mumia Abu Jamal, and Jamil Abdullah Al-Amin (H. Rap Brown), Rev. Joy Powell – Jericho Movement, 2024) further contribute to these individuals' trauma as well as the Black community who loves and supports them. Experiences in the hole, or solitary holding unit (SHU), for months and years, starvation, inadequate medical care, and at times, organized sexual assaults and killings, are among the institutionalized violent practices by prison guards and correctional officers toward Black Freedom Fighters and other incarcerated people (Burton, 2023; Durden-Smith, 1976; Jackson, 1971/1990). Bukhari (2010) reminds us that PTSD was a common response of Black Panthers and BLA members who endured the colonial war waged by the U.S. government. As we make sense and find solutions to the economic, mental, emotional, and/or social challenges of Black people in the United States, experiences of contextual and institutionalized colonial violence must be considered.

In sum, the police, as a state-sanctioned organization, must be understood in its rightful context of Colonialism and Institutionalized Violence in the United States and abroad. As a result of the police history manifesting during Colonialism of the Indigenous and the Chattel Enslavement of Africans in the United States, only to transform to a "public" institution to repress, neutralize, and disrupt the resistance and organizing of *undocumented* European migrants, it becomes clear that the police department was not established to keep safe and protect the common citizenry, but to maintain the status quo, invested interest, and social control for the Class Ruling Elite. If this was the origin of the police, and further included the onslaught and killings by police of Black, Brown, and Indigenous Freedom Fighters historically, as well as the contemporary epidemic of police killings of common people (i.e., average 1,000 police killings per year in the United States), then we can conclude that the police as an institution are grounded and maintained by a legacy as the purveyors of violence, the domestic military wing of the U.S. government. Their ability to take lives with impunity and justification are shields and protections that reflect their political and social positionality. While making sense of the purpose of policing in the United States, which can be understood in some terms in this literature review, it becomes further necessary that we explore and understand the lived experiences of survivors of loved ones killed by police, primarily youth victims.

Thus, the purpose of this book is to highlight the experiences and meanings of the family and loved ones of youth killed by police. Utilizing in-depth and public interviews as primary tools for data collection, this qualitative project sought to deepen our understanding regarding the impact of youth killed by police on survivors. The family and friends of youth victims, including mothers, siblings, aunts and uncles, friends, journalists, attorneys, as well as community activists, contributed their stories and narratives that brought forth this book. We are sincerely indebted, grateful, and privileged to have met, shared space, and learned from all participants.

In the following chapters, our experiences and approaches in collecting the stories of family and community members of youth killed by police are discussed. We further present these narratives, as well as our interpretations of them, in the following chapters. We conclude the book with a discussion of major themes derived from the narratives, while connecting them to existing literature. Moreover, we highlight the project's limitations and solutions to address them, while extending recommendations for everyday people to continue the struggle to challenge and abolish the epidemic of police killings of people in the United States, primarily youth.

References

Abu-Jamal, M. (2016). *We Want Freedom: A Life in the Black Panther Party*. Common Notions: Brooklyn, NY.

Abu-Jamal, M., & Vittoria, S. (2018). *Murder Incorporated Empire, Genocide, and Manifest Destiny. Book One: Dreaming of Empire*. Prison Radio: San Francisco, CA.

Alexander, M. (2012). *The New Jim Crow: Mass Incarceration in the Age of Colorblindness*. New Press: New York, NY.

Baddeley, J. L., Williams, J., L., Rynearson, T., Correa, F., Saindon, C., & Rheingold, A. A. (2015). Death thoughts and images in treatment-seekers after violent loss. *Death Studies*, *39*, 84–91. https://doi.org/10.1080/07481187.2014.893274.

Balko, R. (2006). *Overkill: The Rise of Paramilitary Police Raids in America*. Cato Institute: Washington, DC. Retrieved from https://www.cato.org/white-paper/overkill-rise-paramilitary-police-raids-america.

Baude, W. (2020). Precedent and discretion. *Supreme Court Review*, *313*. Retrieved from https://chicagounbound.uchicago.edu/cgi/viewcontent.cgi?article=13964&context=journal_articles.

Bennett Jr., L. (1965). *Confrontation: Black and White* (1st ed.). Johnson Printing Company: Rochester, MN.

Bies, K. J. (2017). Let the sunshine in: Illuminating the powerful role police unions play in shielding officer misconduct. *Stanford Law & Policy Review*, *28*(1), 109-[vi].

Blackman, D. (2008). *Slavery by Another Name: The Re-Enslavement of Black Americans from the Civil War to World War II*. Anchor Books: New York, NY.

Bobb, M. (2003). Civilian oversight of the police in the United States. *Saint Louis University Public Law Review*, *22*(1), 151–166.

Boelen, P. A., Keijser, J. D., & Smid, G. (2015). Cognitive–behavioral variables mediate the impact of violent loss on post-loss psychopathology. *Psychological Trauma: Theory, Research, Practice, and Policy*, *7*(4), 382–390.

Bogensperger, J., & Lueger-Schuster, B. (2014). Losing a child: Finding meaning in bereavement. *European Journal of Psychotraumatology*, *5*(1), 1–9. https://doi.org/10.3402/ejpt.v5.22910.

Bukhari, S. (2010). *The War Before: The True Life Story of Becoming a Black Panther, Keeping the Faith in Prison & Fighting for Those Left Behind*. The Feminist Press: New York, NY.

Burden-Stelly, C. (2023). *Black Scare/Red Scare: Theorizing Capitalist Racism in the United States*. The University of Chicago Press: Chicago, IL.

Burton, O. (2023). *Tip of the Spear: Black Radicalism, Prison Repression, and the Long Attica Revolt.* University of California Press: Oakland, CA.
Charles, P. J. (2025). *Second Amendment.* Encyclopedia Britannica. Retrieved from https://www.britannica.com/topic/Second-Amendment.
DeGruy, J. (2005). *Post Traumatic Slave Syndrome: America's Legacy of Enduring Injury and Healing.* Joy DeGruy Publications, Inc.: Portland, OR.
Denderen, M. V., Keijser, J. D., Stewart, R., & Boelen, P. A. (2017). Treating complicated grief and posttraumatic stress in homicidally bereaved individuals: A randomized controlled trial. *Clinical Psychology and Psychotherapy, 25*(4), 497–508.
Djelantik, M. J., Smid, G. E., Kleber, R. J., & Boelen, P. A. (2017). Symptoms of prolonged grief, post-traumatic stress, and depression after loss in a Dutch community sample: A latent class analysis. *Psychiatry Research, 247*, 276–281. http://dx.doi.org/10.1016/j.psychres.2016.11.023.
Dog, M. C., & Erdoes, R. (1991). *Lakota Woman.* Harper Perennial: New York, NY.
Dohrn, Z. A. (Executive Producer). (2022). *Mother Country Radicals: A Family History of the Weather Underground* [Audio Podcast]. Crooked Media. Retrieved from https://crooked.com/podcast-series/mother-country-radicals/
Du Bois, W. E. B. (1935). *Black Reconstruction: An Essay Toward a History of the Part Which Black Folk Played in the Attempt to Reconstruct Democracy in America, 1860–1880.* Quinn & Boden Company: Rahway, NJ.
Dunbar-Ortiz, R. (2015). *An Indigenous Peoples' History of the United States.* Beacon Press Books: Boston, MA.
Durden-Smith, J. (1976). *Who Killed George Jackson?* Alfred A. Knopf: New York, NY.
Enck-Wanzer, D. (2010). *The Young Lords: A Reader.* New York University Press: New York, NY.
Fanon, F. (2004). *Colonial War and Mental Disorders.* In Fanon, F. (Eds.), *The Wretched of the Earth* (pp. 181–218). Grove Press: New York, NY.
Fegley, T. (2020). Police unions and officer privileges. *The Independent Review, 25*(2), 165–186.
Fisk, C. L., & Richardson, L. (2017). Police unions. *George Washington Law Review, 85*(3), 712–799.
Goldman, P. L. (1979). *The Death and Life of Malcolm X.* University of Illinois Press: Chicago, IL.
Halvorson, J. T. (2022). *The Impact of Police Unions on the Prosecution of Officers, Legitimacy, and Reform.* Southern Illinois University Carbondale, OpenSIUC: Carbondale. Retrieved from https://opensiuc.lib.siu.edu/gs_rp.
Heeke, C., Kampisiou, C., Niemeyer, H., & Knaevelsrud, C. (2017). A systematic review and meta-analysis of correlates of prolonged grief disorder in adults exposed to violent loss, *European Journal of Psychotraumatology, 8*(6), 1583524. https://doi.org/10.1080/20008198.2019.1583524.
Hess, P. (2000). *Overturning the Culture of Violence.* Burning Spear Publication: St. Petersburg, FL.
Hill, G. (2010). *500 Years of Indigenous Resistance.* PM Press: Oakland, CA.
Huang, L. (2018). *Unmet Needs and Service Satisfaction of Victim Support for the Direct and Indirect Victims of Serious Violence: Results from a Cross-Sectional Survey in Taiwan.* https://doi.org/10.1371/journal.
IBWL21.org. (2024). *Quotes by Dr. John Henry Clark.* Retrieved from https://www.brainyquote.com/authors/john-henrik-clarke-quotes.
Jackson, G. (1971/1990). *Blood in My Eye.* Black Class Press: Baltimore, MD.
James, J. (2024). *Beyond Cop Cities: Dismantling State and Corporate-Funded Armies and Prisons.* Pluto Press: Las Vegas, NV.

Jericho Movement. (2024). Jericho Movement. *Prisoners*. Retrieved from https://www.thejerichomovement.com/.
Kaltman, S., & Bonanno, G. A. (2001). Trauma and bereavement: Examining the impact of sudden and violent deaths. *Anxiety Disorders, 17,* 131–147.
Kondo, Z. A. (1993). *Conspiracys: Unravelling the Assassination of Malcolm X.* Nubia Press: Washington, DC.
Kraska, P. (2007). Militarization and policing: Its relevance to 21st century police. *Policing*, pp. 1–13. https://doi.org/10.1093/police/pam065.
Lambert, L. (2024). Weather underground: American militant group. *Encyclopedia Britannica.* Retrieved from https://www.britannica.com/topic/Weathermen. Accessed 22 August 2024.
Lazu, J. (2013). The Chicago Young Lords: (Re) constructing knowledge and revolution. *Centro Journal, 25*(11), 28–60.
Lichtenthal, W. G., Joseph, M. C., Robert, A. N., & Keesee, N. J. (2010). Sense and significance: A mixed methods examination of meaning making after the loss of one's child. *Journal of Clinical Psychology, 66*(7), 791–812.
Mapping Police Violence. (2024). *Data.* Reviewed and Retrieved on 2/12/24, from https://mappingpoliceviolence.org/?gclid=Cj0KCQiAq5meBhCyARIsAJrtdr50wA0FuRzvDKZ9_faC6z-SRch3Q0G9SckiAHu68Pg1FgMv4ceBxzMaAsBAEALw_wcB.
McKesson, D., Sinyangwe, S., Elzie, J., & Packnett, B. (2016). Police union contracts and police bill of rights analysis. *Campaign Zero.* Retrieved from https://campaignzero.org/wp-content/uploads/2022/11/CampaignZeroPoliceUnionContractReport–1.pdf.
Meko, H. (2024). N.Y.P.D. misconduct settlements cost $500 million over 6 years. *The New York Times.* Retrieved from https://www.nytimes.com/2024/02/29/nyregion/nypd-police-misconduct-settlements.html#:~:text=The%20board%20said%20it%20had,also%20take%20years%20to%20resolve.
Morin, R., Parker, K., Stepler, R., & Mercer, A. (2017). *Behind the Badge: Amid Protest Calls for Reform, How Police View Their Jobs, Key Issues and Recent Fatal Encounters Between Blacks and Police.* Pew Research Center. Retrieved from https://www.pewresearch.org/wp-content/uploads/sites/20/2017/01/Police-Report_FINAL_web.pdf.
Mosvick, N. (2021). Looking back at the Ku Klux Klan act. *National Constitution Center.* Retrieved from https://constitutioncenter.org/blog/looking-back-at-the-ku-klux-klan-act.
Muntaqim, J. (2020). *We Are Our Own Liberators.* Black Dragon Multimedia Management Enterprise: Rochester, NY.
Nakajima, S., Masaya, I., Akemi, S., Takako, K., & Konishi, T. (2012). Complicated grief in those bereaved by violent death: The effects of post-traumatic stress disorder on complicated grief. *Dialogues in Clinical Neuroscience, 14*(2), 210–214.
NDN Collective. (2025). *Leonard Peltier Released After 49 Years of Wrongful Incarceration.* Retrieved on 06/19/2025, from https://ndncollective.org/leonard-peltier-released-from-49-years-of-wrongful-incarceration/.
Nickerson, A., Liddell, B. J., Maccallum, F., Steel, Z., Silove, D., & Bryant, R. (2014). Posttraumatic stress disorder and prolonged grief in refugees exposed to trauma and loss. *Biomed Central Psychiatry, 14*(106), 1–11. https://doi.org/10.1186/1471-244X-14–106.
Outland, R. (2019). Symbolic meaning of violence: Urban African-American adolescent males' perspectives. *Journal of African American Studies, 23,* 233–255.
Outland, R., Noel, T., Rounsville, K., Boatwright, T., Waleed, C., & Abraham, A. (2020). Living with trauma: Impact of police killings on the lives of the family

and community of child and teen victims. *Current Psychology, 41*, 7059–7073. Retrieved from https://rdcu.be/cbkti.

Palante. (1970). Palante! *Latin Revolutionary News Service, 2*(8). Retrieved from https://content.wisconsinhistory.org/digital/collection/p15932coll8/id/82011.

Place, N. (2018). Double due process: How police unions and law enforcement bills of rights enable police violence and prevent accountability. *University of San Francisco Law Review, 52*(2), 275–298.

Redvers, N., Aubrey, P., Celidwen, Y., & Hill, K. (2023). Indigenous peoples: Traditional knowledges, climate change, and health. *PLoS Global Public Health, 3*(10). https://doi.org/10.1371/journal.pgph.0002474. Retrieved from https://pmc.ncbi.nlm.nih.gov/articles/PMC10575522/.

Rheingold, A. A., Baddeley, J. L., Williams, J. L., Brown, C., Wallace, M. M., Correa, F., & Rynearson, E. K. (2015). Restorative retelling for violent death: An investigation of treatment effectiveness, influencing factors, and durability. *Journal of Loss and Trauma, 20*, 541–555.

Rheingold, A. A., & Williams, J. L. (2018). Module-based comprehensive approach for addressing heterogeneous mental health sequelae of violent loss survivors. *Death Studies, 42*(3), 164–171. https://doi.org/10.1080/07481187.2017.1370798.

Rheingold, A. A., Zinzow, H., Hawkins, A., Saunders, B. E., & Kilpatrick, D. G. (2012). Prevalence and mental health outcomes of homicide survivors in a representative US sample of adolescents: Data from the 2005 national survey of adolescents. *Journal of Child Psychology and Psychiatry, 53*(6), 687–694.

Roberts, D. (1997). *Killing the Black Body: Race, Reproduction, and the Meaning of Liberty*. Random House: New York, NY.

Rodney, W. (1969/1996). *The Grounding With My Brothers*. Research Associates School Times Publications: Chicago, IL.

Rodney, W. (1982). *How Europe Underdeveloped Africa*. Howard University Press: Washington, DC.

Rodriquez, D. (2023). Chapter 12: The obsolescence of 'police brutality': Counterinsurgency in a moment of police reform. In Cunneen, C., Deckert, A., Porter, A., Tauri, J., & Webb, R. (Eds.), *The Routledge International Handbook on Decolonizing Justice*. Routledge: New York, NY.

Rushin, S. (2015). Structural reform litigation in American police departments. *Minnesota Law Review, 99*(4), 1343–1422.

Saindon, C., Rheingold, A., A., Baddeley, J., Wallace, M. M., Brown, C., & Rynearson, E., K. (2014). Restorative retelling for violent loss: An open clinical trial. *Death Studies, 38*, 251–258. https://doi.org/10.1080/07481187.2013.783654.

Schuttler, J. F. (1991). The American Indian movement as a revolutionary organization. *Student Thesis, Dissertations, & Professional Papers No. 9337*. Retrieved from https://scholarworks.umt.edu/etd/9337.

Schweikert, J. R. (2020). Qualified immunity: A legal, practical, and moral failure. *Cato Institute, Policy Analysis No. 901*. Retrieved from https://papers.ssrn.com/sol3/papers.cfm?abstract_id=3694725.

Seale, B. (1991). *Seize The Time. A Story of the Black Panther Party and Huey P. Newton*. Black Classic Press: Baltimore, MD.

Shakur, M. (2011). *Justice and Amnesty: Applying the South African Truth and Reconciliation Process to the North American Black Liberation Movement*. Truth and Reconciliation Commission in the United States. Retrieved from https://mutulushakur.com/wp-content/uploads/2014/03/TRC-booklet.pdf.

Simonson, J. (2021). Police reform through a power lens. *Yale Law Journal, 130*(4), 778–861.

Sloan, C. (2005). Bastards of the party. *Documentary*. Retrieved from https://www.imdb.com/title/tt0455913/.

Smid, G. E., Kleber, R. J., de la Rie, S. M., Bos, J. B. A., Gersons, B. P. R., & Boelen, P. A. (2015). Brief eclectic psychotherapy for traumatic grief (BEP-TG): Toward integrated treatment of symptoms related to traumatic loss. *European Journal of Psychotraumatology*, *6*(1), 27324. https://doi.org/10.3402/ejpt.v6.27324.

Staggers-Hakim, R. (2016). The nation's unprotected children and the ghost of Mike Brown, or the impact of national police killings on the health and social development of African American boys. *Journal of Human Behavior in the Social Environment*, *26*(3–4), 390–399.

Stiles, K. (2020). The long term effect of bereavement and grief with a highly-publicized violent death. *Journal of Loss and Trauma*. https://doi.org/10.1080/15325024.2020.1727670.

Strohlic, N. (2014). *The 14 Black Teens Killed by Cops Since Michael Brown*. Retrieved from https://www.thedailybeast.com/the-14-teens-killed-by-cops-since-michael-brown.

Umoja, A. O. (2013). *We Will Shoot Back: Armed Resistance in the Mississippi Freedom Movement*. New York University Press: New York, NY.

USA Facts Team. (2025). Which states have the highest police officer salaries? *USA Facts*. Retrieved from https://usafacts.org/articles/which-states-have-the-highest-police-officer-salaries/.

UTEP Connect (University of Texas El Paso). (2023). Highest paying criminal justice jobs in 2023. *Extended University*. Retrieved from https://www.utep.edu/extendeduniversity/utepconnect/blog/december-2023/highest-paying-criminal-justice-jobs.html.

Vitale, A. S. (2018). *The End of Policing*. Verso: New York, NY.

Wells, I. B. (1970/2020). *Crusade for Justice: The Autobiography of Ida B. Wells* (2nd ed.). University of Chicago Press.

Whitaker, M. (2023). *Saying It Loud: 1966-The Year Black Power Challenged the Civil Rights Movement*. Simon & Schuster: New York, NY.

Williams, S. T. (2007). *Blue Rage, Black Redemption: A Memoir*. Touchstone, Simon & Schuster, Inc.: New York, NY.

Workers of the World. (2020, December 17). *Fred Hampton Talks Anarchists, SDS, Weathermen, and the White Working Class* [Video]. Youtube. Retrieved from https://www.youtube.com/watch?v=uoRV3LeD_BE&t=79s.

WPR, World Population Review. (2023). *Police Killings by Country 2024*. Retrieved from https://worldpopulationreview.com/country-rankings/police-killings-by-country.

Wright, T. R., Carr, C. N., & Gasek, J. W. P. (2022). Truth and reconciliation: The Ku Klux Klan hearings of 1871 and the genesis of section 1983. *Dickinson Law Review*, *685*. Retrieved from https://ideas.dickinsonlaw.psu.edu/dlr/vol126/iss3/2.

3

GROUNDINGS WITH FAMILIES AND COMMUNITIES OF YOUTH KILLED BY POLICE

Designing Their Stories

Research Design

Based on the number of children and teens killed by police per state in 2016/2017, and the proximity of the state from the research team's location (Brockport/Rochester, NY), two states, one in Midwest and one in West Coast of the United States, were selected for this research. Specifically, 17 youth victims were killed by police in Southern California (Los Angeles [LA] and surrounding cities), and eight in Chicago, Illinois during the abovementioned time frame. This qualitative study was exploratory in nature, in which it sought to understand the lived experiences of the family and loved ones of children and teens killed by police (Marshall & Rossman, 2011). This study utilized an in-depth interview design to explore the impact of police killings on the lived experiences of participants.

Settings

The study took place in five cities and two states on the West Coast and in the Midwest United States. In-depth interviews were conducted in a private or public setting (e.g., personal office, restaurant parking lot, interviewees' home, neighborhood parks, and a funeral home and cemetery) according to participants' choosing. Public interviews were conducted in public spaces, which included public parks, gas stations, as well as neighborhood sidewalks and parking lots. The locations for public interviews were determined according to two factors: 1) Youth victims' neighborhood and 2) the location where the youth killing by police occurred. The research team agreed

DOI: 10.4324/9781003665915-3

that friends, neighbors, and associates of youth victims in both locations were possibly impacted by the youth homicide by police. Thus, it was necessary to capture the narratives of all survivors in these locations. In addition, all interviews were conducted during business hours in attempts to ensure the team's safety while traveling with heavy and valuable equipment.

Participants

Twenty-four participants were involved in this study: 16 in-depth interviewees and 8 public interviewees. The racial demographics of in-depth interviewees included 1 White, 3 Hispanics, and 12 African Americans. The gender of these individuals were nine males and seven females. Their ages were between 18 and 60 years, which included three young (18–34), ten middle (35–49), and three older (50 and older) adults. In-depth interviewees' relation to youth victims included three mothers, an aunt, a cousin, and two friends, along with five activists, a college professor, two lawyers, and one reporter.

In regard to the racial and gender makeup of the eight public interviewees, only African American males participated in public interviews. Their relation to the victim included friends and neighbors, as well as residents who live in the deceased youth's community and the location where the youth homicides by police occurred. It must be noted that participants self-reported the abovementioned demographics during interviews when describing their history and backgrounds, which in turn, was documented by the interviewers. As a result, participant inclusion criteria for this study were the following: *1) Family or loved one of child or teen victim of police killings from January 2016 to August 2017 (e.g., relative, neighbor, classmate, teacher, and friend of victims) and 2) child or teen victim's death had a direct impact on their daily life.*

Participant Recruitment

This study utilized a step-by-step guide for participant recruitment. During step one, a team member identified the name, age, gender, location of child/teen victim, and news articles about the death. This information was readily available in the Excel spreadsheet of children and teen victims. Victim information was also readily available on the website killedbypolice.net. Step two consisted of gathering as much information about the victim as possible. This information included the victim's address, neighborhood, school, friends, family members, and neighbors. After gathering this information, step three included creating a list of possible participants' contact information. Information about possible participants was gathered while searching a range of web links for news articles, videos, and archives about the victim's death by police. This list provided the team an idea of the approximate number of participants for each victim (e.g., eight possible participants for a single victim) and the best strategy for contacting participants (e.g., phone, email, Twitter, and Facebook). A total of 17 youth victims were identified between two states, including Southern California and Chicago, Illinois. The age range of youth victims killed by police in 2016/2017 was between 9 and 19 years, with an average age of 16 years. Of the 17 victims, participants in this study were representative of 9 of these deceased youth. Thus, the sample population represented the majority of youth killed by police (9 of 17, 52.94 %) in two states.

Step four consisted of team members deciding if a participant met the inclusion criteria. If determined yes, step five consisted of altering the script for contacting a participant, if necessary. During step six, a member of the team contacted a possible participant to determine the individual's willingness to partake in the study. Possible participants were contacted via social media networks, including Facebook (e.g., Messenger), Twitter, and LinkedIn, as well as by email and phone. The pool of potential in-depth interviewees included 273 contacts from two states. These contacts included the deceased youth's family, friends, and loved ones; community residents and service providers; and police officers and city officials (i.e., Mayor of Los Angeles, CA and Chicago, IL). Of the 273 contacts, 22 individuals agreed to partake in the in-depth interviews. Due to time allotted between the team's travel from state to state and in-depth interviews, six individuals withdrew from the study. As a result, 16 in-depth interviewees participated in the study, with a total response rate of 5.86% (16 of 273). If a participant volunteered to be part of the study, step seven included scheduling a time, date, and location for the interview. In-depth interviews were scheduled according to participant's availability, convenience, and comfort in space (e.g., a participant's home versus the public library). Step eight consisted of logging participant's contact information to an Excel spreadsheet. Step nine involved a team member writing a short field note about the interaction with the participant. Finally, step ten included the researcher repeating steps four through ten with a different possible participant.

Sampling Frame and Sampling

This study used purposeful sampling as the sampling frame. Purposeful sampling "provides context-rich and detailed accounts of specific populations and locations" (Ravitch & Carl, 2021, p. 83). Furthermore, purposeful sampling allows the researchers to "deliberately select individuals because of their unique ability to answer a study's research questions" (Ravitch & Carl, 2021, p. 83). Thus, purposeful sampling allowed the researchers to recruit and select participants based on their experiences, knowledge of the child/teen victims' murders, and proximity to the study site locations (Patton, 2002; Ravitch & Carl, 2021).

Snowball Sampling

This study used a snowball sampling approach to recruit participants. Specifically, this approach involved identifying cases of interest from people who knew people were information-rich (Mack et al., 2005; Marshall & Rossman, 2011). Thus, participants who completed public interviews informed others who met the inclusion criteria about the study, yielding an additional four participants. Snowball sampling required minimal time and provided researchers the opportunity to engage directly with referred participants, given that they were associates of in-depth interviewees. During snowball sampling, all individuals who referred others for the study were encouraged to maintain the privacy of their participation in this research. In other words, a team member encouraged interviewees not to disclose their participation

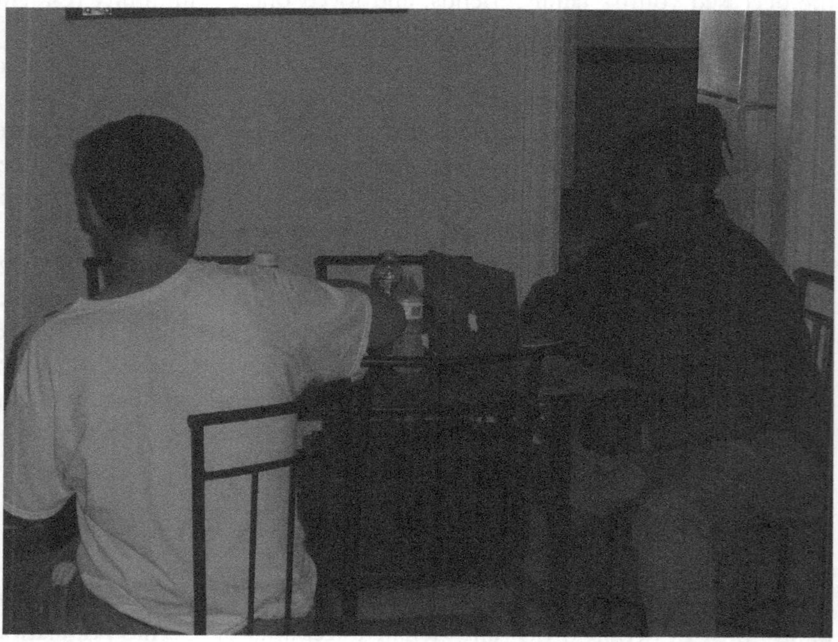

FIGURE 3.1 Researchers' Kris Rounsville (left) and Thomas Noel, Jr. (right) sharing laughs and support following a long day Of Field work in Capital Heights, MD.

in the study when making referrals. Snowball sampling allowed researchers access to potential participants that the team typically may not have had access to during the study. As a result, this strategy provided the team access (Mack et al., 2005) to some of the family, friends, and community members of deceased youths that are rarely mentioned in media news reports, articles, and social media outlets.

Finally, the utility of snowball sampling provided the team access to a *hidden* population of people who may be unwilling or hesitant to reveal their identities and participate in the study (Mack et al., 2005; Naderifar et al., 2017) given the sensitive nature and phenomenon of the research. Furthermore, successful implementation of snowball sampling was largely dependent on the researchers' abilities to demonstrate and convey honesty, transparency, openness, and ultimately trust to participants (i.e., the loved ones of youth victims of police terrorism and violence). The absence of these criteria and characteristics in snowball sampling and in qualitative research methods in general challenges the authentic validity of the overall investigation of critical phenomena and the study (Naderifar et al., 2017).

Procedures

All procedures in this study followed ethical standards of the national Institutional Review Board (IRB) and were approved by the IRB committee at a College in Upstate NY. After receiving IRB approval, the research team used an eight-week period to contact and recruit participants and to collect data for this study. Specifically, weeks one and two were dedicated to gathering the contact information of the friends and loved ones of youth victims of police killings. Weeks three through five were devoted to contacting participants and scheduling a time and date to meet. A team member contacted participants via phone and or email. Scheduling for travel arrangements occurred during week six. The research team used weeks seven and eight to travel to different cities and states to conduct in-depth interviews with the family and loved ones of youth victims of police violence. In addition, public interviews with friends, neighbors, and community members of the deceased youth occurred during these visits. During all in-depth and public interviews, at least two researchers were present. For clarity, participants who completed the in-depth interviews differed from those who partook in the public ones. On the one hand, in-depth interviews were scheduled prior to the team's visit. On the other hand, the team made contact with public interviewees during the team's visit to the community of the deceased youth. Informed consent was obtained from all participants in the study.

FIGURE 3.2 Researcher Rafael Outland taking a picture of an overlook in Capital Heights, MD.

Data Collection

In-depth Interview

The research team used in-depth interviews for data collection. These interviews allowed researchers the opportunity to capture the essence and meaning of participants' experiences in their own words. Specifically, in-depth interviews assisted team members in understanding the meaning of losing a loved one to police violence (Marshall & Rossman, 2011). The research team used a topical or guided approach to develop questions for the interview protocol. This approach allowed the team to explore a few general topics to help uncover participants' views but otherwise respected individuals' frames and structures of their narratives (Marshall & Rossman, 2011). Sensitizing concepts used to help frame the interview protocol for this study included *police killings, impact, family and loved ones of children and teen victims, and aftermath.* Informed consent was obtained from all individual participants included in the study. A total of 16 in-depth interviews were conducted, in which the team anticipated conducting 20. In-depth interviews with adults ranged from 45 to 70 minutes. At least two team members were present during in-depth interviews with adults. In-depth interviews took place at locations most convenient for participants, including, but not limited to, their homes, church, school, personal office, or public location. Family, friends, and neighbors of the deceased youth, as well as community service providers, participated in the in-depth interviews.

Observations: Public Interviews

The research team also used observations for data collection in this study. Observations during qualitative research typically involve the systematic noting of events and behaviors of participants and the researcher, in a social setting. Observations in this study included a variety of activities by the research team, such as spending time at participants' homes and communities, becoming acquainted with participants' daily lives, and learning how to record and take note of actions and interactions of participants (Marshall & Rossman, 2011). Friends and loved ones who resided in the community of the deceased youth and/or lived in the neighborhood where the police killing took place were involved in public interviews. The team conducted a total of eight public interviews. During in-depth and public interviews, observations played an important role for the team to monitor the body language, affect, and tone of voice of participants. The research team did not collect identifying information of public interviewees. Thus, no one, not even team members, had access to this information of public interviewees. All members of the research team recorded field notes of our observations. Field notes are researchers' detailed, nonjudgmental, concrete descriptions of their observations (Marshall & Rossman, 2011). Field notes derived from this study were included as part of the final dataset prior to the start of data analysis.

All in-depth and public interviews were audio and video recorded. Specifically, all in-depth interviewees agreed to have their interviews video and audio recorded. Moreover, two public interviewees, one in Southern CA and one in Chicago, IL, chose not to have their interviews audio or video recorded. During these instances, a team member acted as the designated note taker during interviews. Specifically, the team member attempted to jot down participants' narratives verbatim or used the words of interviewees. These notes were later added to the archive of data for review during data analysis. The research team transcribed and analyzed notes recorded during interviews in order to identify meaningful codes and themes.

Data Management and Analysis

All audio and video recordings were stored on an external hard drive with an encrypted password. The external hard drive was kept in a lockbox in the principal investigator's office. The research team used an eight-week period to analyze, interpret, and synthesize the data. Specifically, the research team used a grounded theory approach for data analysis. This approach consisted of the research team developing meaningful codes, categories, and themes that were derived from participants' narratives (Charmaz, 2014). The research team met once a month via online portals (e.g., Zoom and Skype) to analyze and discuss meaningful codes and themes from the interviews and was involved in ongoing email threads during this time. Moreover, the team wrote analytic memos related to meaningful codes, themes, and categories that were derived during data analysis (Charmaz, 2014). These memos were circulated among team members, which members provided and received feedback about their determined codes and themes. This process has been described as member checking (Charmaz, 2014).

Grounded Theory

Grounded theory approaches consist of systematic, yet flexible, guidelines for collecting and analyzing qualitative data to construct theories from the data themselves (Charmaz, 2014). From early pioneers, such as Glaser (1978) and Strauss (1987), to recent scholars such as Charmaz (2014), grounded theorists carry the belief that systematic qualitative analysis consists of its own logic that produces theory. As a result, this study utilized a systematic approach for data analysis, with the intent of producing a theoretical framework that was derived from the data. Moreover, the team used the following grounded theory approaches for data analysis: Initial coding, focused coding, and theoretical sampling.

Initial Coding

During the initial coding process, team members coded participants' narratives, from in-depth and public interviews. Team members utilized block coding during the first round of the coding process. Block coding consisted of a team member jotting down short phrases or statements that represented several sentences or phrases of participants' comments (Charmaz, 2014). All codes from team members were compiled in a single list. The list consisted of more than 442 individual codes. The list was reviewed by all team members to determine if the codes were accurate representations of participants' statements.

Focused Coding

The second phase of data analysis consisted of focused coding. Focused coding consists of using the most meaningful and/or frequent codes to move through the process of data analysis. Focused codes tend to advance the theoretical framing of a study, in which these codes tend to be more conceptual and poignant to the researcher's interpretation of participants' narratives (Charmaz, 2014). During the first phase of focused coding, team members collectively reviewed the coding list, in which a yellow and green color scheme was used to determine the most meaningful and/or frequent codes. Step two consisted of members placing codes marked with the above-mentioned colors on a separate list. Sixty-three of the 442 codes were placed on the new list. Next, step three consisted of team members categorizing codes from the list according to similarities and/or identical codes. Finally, step four involved team members collectively conceptualizing categories and meaningful codes into a thematic scheme. Gerund phrases and short words were used to capture the essence of each category and its given theme. This process produced a set of themes and subthemes that were grounded in participants' narratives, or the data themselves (Charmaz, 2014).

Theoretical Sampling

After establishing a set of themes and subthemes that represented participants' narratives, step three involved the process of theoretical sampling. This process can be defined as a researcher's use of derived themes and subthemes to check their validity and accuracy vis-à-vis the data and literature (Charmaz, 2014). Thus, team members were assigned specific themes and subthemes, and then sifted through the research literature and participants' narratives to determine their accuracy. Following this process, team members determined that some themes and subthemes were more consistent than others. As a result, the team decided on which themes and subthemes would be presented in this book based on three factors: 1) themes and subthemes captured the essence of participants' narratives; 2) themes and subthemes were consistent with the literature; and 3) team members' shared consensus.

The following section includes a presentation of the stories and experiences of family and community members of youth killed by police. These narratives, coupled with major themes and researchers' interpretation, capture the essence of what it means to lose a child to police violence. In addition, we discuss and make sense of the connection between major themes and past literature. Finally, we provide recommendations and strategies that can be used by everyday people to combat police killings in their local community, as well as limitations of the project and strategies to address them.

References

Charmaz, K. (2014). *Constructing Grounded Theory.* Sage Publications: London, UK.

Glaser, B. G. (1978). *Theoretical Sensitivity: Advances in the Methodology of Grounded Theory.* The Sociology Press.

Mack, N., Woodsong, C., Macqueen, K., Guest, G., & Namey, E. (2005). *Qualitative Research Methods: A Data Collector's Field Guide.* Family Health International.

Marshall, C., & Rossman, G. B. (2011). *Designing Qualitative Research* (5th ed.). Sage Publications: Los Angeles, CA.

Naderifar, M., Goli, H., & Ghaljaie, F. (2017). Snowball sampling: A purposeful method of sampling in qualitative research. *Strides in Development of Medical Education, 14*, e67670. https://doi.org/10.5812/sdme.67670.

Patton, M. Q. (2002). *Qualitative Research and Evaluation Methods* (3rd ed.). Sage Publications: Thousand Oaks, CA.

Ravitch, S. M., & Carl, N. M. (2021). *Qualitative Research: Bridging the Conceptual, Theoretical, and Methodological* (2nd ed.). Sage Publications: Thousand Oaks, CA.

Strauss, A. L. (1987). *Qualitative Analysis for Social Scientists.* Cambridge University Press.

4

THEIR STORIES MATTER

Lessons From the Family and Community of Youth Killed by Police

The purpose of this project was to understand the impact of police killings on the family and community of children and teen victims. The goal of this work was to shed light on the meaning and essence of losing a loved one to police violence. A major hope was that participants' narratives can be useful for activists and service providers 1) to bring about justice for youth victims and families, 2) to hold police officers accountable for the untimely murder of a child or teen, and 3) to conjure necessary resources and support for survivors of youth homicide by police. In order to humanize the experiences and narratives of survivors of youth killed by police, the following section provides a brief introduction of the participants. In addition, major themes and interpretations of them, along with interviewees' supporting narratives, are presented.

Participant Introduction

Family and Friends of Youth Victims

Precious Sasser, mother of four loving children, experienced the traumatic and untimely death of her son, Kenny Watkins, by police violence. Specifically, as a teen mother, Ms. Sasser acknowledged that Kenny was always a part of her life and further identified him as "my guy" due to his radiant personality and "beautiful smile." She described him as being "well known and loved by his peers" and held in high esteem by former teachers, mentors, and sports coaches. As a big brother to three younger siblings, Ms. Sasser believed that her son set a positive example for his siblings based on

DOI: 10.4324/9781003665915-4

his involvement and passion for the arts and athletics. She stated that Kenny was more than a young Black male who was "shot in 20 seconds" by an undercover Los Angeles Police Department (LAPD) officer while riding his bike on the sidewalk, but was a beacon of light for his family, friends, and community.

Who is Ms. Nicole? Ms. Nicole, African American woman in her mid-40s, is a native of Denver, CO and has resided in Chicago, IL for most of her life, which she calls "home." She is a mother of four children, two of whom were killed by gun violence in Chicago, including Corshawn Lewis, a 17-year-old male who was murdered by Chicago police department (CPD) officers. Following the talk with Ms. Nicole, we learned that she has lived a life filled with trauma and violence after losing a boyfriend (Corshawn's dad) and two sons to gun violence in Chicago's inner city. Despite these losses, Ms. Nicole was warm, welcoming, energetic, and excited to provide the "real" story and experiences of her son in the aftermath of his murder by police.

Who is Lakeisha Brandon? Ms. Brandon, African American female in her late 40s, was born and raised in Chicago, IL. She is the mother of three children, one of whom was murdered by an off-duty Chicago police officer in 2017. Her son's name was Aaron Brandon. Lakeisha learned about the Kids Killed By Police Study (KKBPS) project from her attorney, Victor Henderson. After interviewing Mr. Henderson, he recommended Ms. Brandon as a good candidate for the project, and the team agreed. Due to a pending lawsuit by Ms. Brandon and her attorney against Chicago PD, she was unable to discuss details about the circumstances that led to her son's murder. Nevertheless, Lakeisha provided an important narrative about her son's legacy and the impact of his murder on his family, friends, and community. While observing Ms. Brandon's Love for her children and courage to complete the interview, we further noticed the pain and struggle she carries following the burial of her child.

Who is Cassina Turner? Cassina Turner, African American female in her mid-30s, was born and raised in South Central LA. She became aware of the KKBPS project due to her relationship with Precious, the mother of Black male teen who was killed by police, Kenny Watkins. Ms. Turner possessed a bubbly and vibrant personality. She continued to use humor and jokes to lighten the overall mood and experience of the talk. Her relationship and connection to Precious and her children are the result of a long history of surviving and supporting each other during past experiences of grief and loss. In this regard, she suggested that Precious, Kenny, and his siblings have always been "family," which is reflective of the following: "That's my dog [Precious]. Like we've done everything together. We cried together, we laughed together. When my mom died, she was there. When her granny died . . . I was there for her."

FIGURE 4.1 Community memorial for a youth victim killed by police in Los Angeles, CA.

Who is Jeremy? Jeremy, African American male in his mid-30s, is a native of Los Angeles, CA. He grew up in a low-income urban environment in LA, while attending a suburban school during his childhood and teen years. Jeremy highlighted obstacles during his upbringing that carried the potential to curtail his dreams of becoming a Division 1 athlete, which included dealing with the "bad environment" that can exist in some poor urban settings. Jeremy reminded us during the talk that "plenty of good people live in these spaces . . . and not all people in the ghetto are bad." As a result, he provided important information surrounding his younger cousin, Kenny's legacy and influence on others. Kenny was gunned down by LAPD while biking through a local neighborhood. Jeremy was referred to the KKBPS by his cousin, Precious Sasser, Kenny's mother. Jeremy's story was grounded in his experiences as an older cousin and role model for his younger cousins, including Kenny. He further discussed the ways Kenny touched the hearts and souls of many during his short-lived existence, while denoting the emotional devastation experienced by Kenny's friends, family, and loved ones following his death.

Who is Kai? Kai, a 19-year-old African American female, is a native of Chicago, IL. Her participation in the KKBPS occurred due to the untimely murder of Black male teen, Corshawn Lewis. Corshawn was gunned down by Chicago police officers in an alleyway near his home. After police received a call of a group of teens in an alleyway, CPD arrived and sped by in an unmarked vehicle. The deceased teen *supposedly* fired a gun at the unmarked car, while officers unloaded their weapons, killing the teen on the spot. Kai described herself as a "real friend" to Corshawn and mother of his daughter, who was a tender 1-year-old infant at the time of the interview.

Who is Kimberly? Kimberly, native of South Los Angeles, CA, was a dear friend of Kenny Watkins, 17-year-old Black male who was gunned down while riding his bike by LAPD undercover officers. Kimberly currently resides in LA County, where she remains involved in community and church volunteer services. Her earliest memories of Kenny began as youth in the church, where they shared intergenerational links between their grandmothers. Both grandparents strongly pushed their grandchildren's involvement in church activities, and through these activities, Kimberly and Kenny first established a friendship:

> I remember when we were young in the church, both of our grandmothers brought us to the church. My grandma had been going to that church for years, so she brought me. She wanted me to come to church to start dancing, and ushering, and singing. All of a sudden, Kenny and his family came and we just clicked.

Community Members of Youth Victims

Activists Introduction

Mr. Jesse Smith, 45-year-old African American male, is a native of Palmdale, CA, a neighboring community 20 miles from LA. Jesse has remained involved in pastoral work and activism with low-income young men from the community. In the last ten years, Mr. Smith's activism consisted of legal fights against the courts and LA County Sheriff in attempts to gain justice for African American community members following encounters of sheriff violence, harassment, and discrimination. He suggested that "The city of Palmdale there were just so many issues of race and injustice as it related to African Americans' opportunities and the way they were treated out here."

Pharaoh Mitchel, 42-year-old African American male, is a native of Los Angeles, CA. He has lived in Antelope Valley, a neighboring region of LA, for the past 15 years. Mr. Mitchell identifies as a community activist of Antelope Valley, which his ideas, strategies, and actions have brought about social and economic justice for countless community members. Pharaoh remains grounded in his positionality as a community activist and remains faithful that activism and community organizing are useful tools to fight the LA Sheriff's and the court's abuses and unlawful practices bestowed on African Americans and Latino residents. He identified such a positionality as *Refusing to sell my soul: One finger salute*, which is reflected in the following: "I like to salute with one finger. My soul is not for sale for anybody. We're not going to back down from our community, we love our community. We are passionate about our community."

Who is Jamie Garcia? Ms. Garcia, a native of South Los Angeles, CA, identifies as a member of the Latinx Community, a nurse, and a community activist. As a Latinx female, she noted that her background and lived challenges provide her a better perspective and understanding of those she serves. According to Ms. Garcia, this critical perspective is one of her greatest assets:

> I think one of the biggest things for me to really embrace and embody being a Latinx female is that where Kenny Watkins was murdered is not my community, right? So I enter from that perspective, really understanding that. And I am not a Black woman either. So I enter into this experience understanding that as well.

Her nursing background extends over ten years of working and serving patients at several hospitals in LA County, in which she is currently a nurse to clients with physical illnesses and challenges. In addition, activism remains an important part of Jamie's identity. To Ms. Garcia, being an activist is *A Way of Life*, and therefore, involves unwavering commitment and dedication to serving others. Through her active involvement in *LA CAN, Skid Row Initiative*, and *the Coalition Against Police Spying*, Jamie believes that activism can serve as a platform for healing through organizing.

Who is Carlos Montes? Carlos, 50–65-year-old Chicano or Latinx male, is a native of East Los Angeles, CA. His parents were born and raised in Mexico, in which they migrated to the United States with Mr. Montes at the tender age of 5. Due to Carlos and his family's historical challenges to attain their rights from local and national government as immigrants to the United States, Carlos believed that these early experiences sparked his passion and desire to join forces with *Centro Community Service Organization (CSO)*, according to the following:

> I'm with Centro, CSO, Community Service Organization . . . and historically our work is fighting for immigrant rights against deportations, against ICE (Immigrant and Customs Enforcement). . . And know your rights and fight for legalization for all.

Who is Dr. David Stovall? Dr. Stovall, African American male, 40+ years old, is a native of Chicago, IL. He currently works as a college professor at a major university in Chicago, alongside his activist work with youth and families. David learned about the KKBPS project from a professional colleague and friend, Dr. Noel, a KKBPS co-researcher. Dr. Stovall expressed advocating for many families in South and West Sides of Chicago with hopes of receiving justice following the killing of their loved one by police. His narrative was grounded in details surrounding the history of repressive policing in Chicago's marginalized communities. Specifically, he discussed past work with Rekia Boyd's family, African American female who was gunned down by off-duty Chicago PDs, as well as his commitment to struggling for equitable conditions for Chicago residents who exist on the margins of poverty.

Critical Lawyers and Reporters Introduction

Jorge Gonzalez, 56-year-old Mexican American, identifies as a criminal attorney in LA County. His parents are natives of Mexico, in which he resided until the tender age of 7 years. Mr. Gonzalez's parents were natives of Novales, Mexico, until eventually migrating to El Paso, Texas. As a result of growing up in a military family and having family ties in both Mexico and the United States, Jorge described his early years in the United States as "being born on the border," which is depicted in the following:

> So I was born on the border, and you know, I have a saying . . . [Spanish language], which means I have one foot here and one foot there. I kind of live in both, half my family down there and half my family over here. In fact, I've had more family move back to Mexico than move to the US.

Mr. Gonzalez spoke in depth regarding his extensive background as a criminal lawyer. He has over 37 years of lawyering experience, which he expressed a desire to exclusively handle Civil Rights cases. This interest was sparked during Jorge's college years in the 1970s. During this period, he described himself as being heavily involved in student activism, primarily in regard to protest against the Vietnam War.

Who is Victor Henderson? Mr. Henderson, African American male in his late 50s, is a native of Chicago, IL. He has practiced law for more than 30 years, which early in his career he primarily dealt with corporate cases and later transitioned to a focus on Civil Rights lawyering. Victor expressed that he lacked the passion and motivation for work as a corporate lawyer, according to the following:

> Prior to becoming a Civil Rights lawyer, or should I say handling Civil Rights cases, I did largely commercial work. Big corporations, the

majority who are owned by wealthy White people and so doing commercial work, I don't think there was the same motivation for people to be dishonest and lie.

Who is Eric Russell? Eric Russell, 40+-year-old African American male, is a native of Chicago, IL. Eric participated in the KKBPS project due to his advocacy work with families impacted by police violence and murder. Mr. Russell's trajectory as an advocate stems from his late aunt's, Margaret Russell, involvement in the Civil Rights movement during the 1960s. Eric recalled experiences of fear and terror as a child during several raids by the *Ku Klux Klan (KKK)*, a White supremacy vigilante terrorist group at his family's residence in Birmingham, Alabama. Remembering this childhood fear and experienced terror of family members were major contributors to Eric's decision to become an advocate for families impacted by police killings.

Who is Zak Koeske? Zak, White male, mid-to-late 30s, is a native of Chicago, IL. He worked for the *Chicago Tribune* newspaper as a crime reporter for the past nine years. Mr. Koeske learned about the KKBPS project through his reporting on the case of Aaron Brandon. Mr. Brandon, a 17-year-old African American male, was shot and killed by an off-duty Chicago PD officer during the sale of a laptop that was arranged online. According to Zak, what led him to investigate the case was based on what he called the officer's "suspicious story" that was released in the news. Mr. Koeske suggested the following: "They put out a press release that said there was this incident where two individuals attempted to rob somebody and the person responded by shooting one of them and the other one got away."

Findings: Family and Friends

Meaning of Losing a "Good Kid"

Meaning of Losing a "Good Kid" was a valued theme in this study. Specifically, a good kid can be defined as a youth blessed with the gift of "making others laugh and feel heard," "creative and artistic," and in constant pursuit of "possessed dreams and ambitions." In addition, most youth victims were involved in sports and social activities, which further catered to their desires and strivings to be productive youth. Losing a good kid involves disruption of close relationships between youth victims and their family, friends, and community. These close relationships, oftentimes, were grounded on principles of Love, Loyalty, and Trust between individuals. Thus, the light that radiated from the heart and souls of youth victims was transformed into dark days for family and friends after their untimely murder by police. For example, Ms. Brandon described her son as follows:

> So, Aaron is a smart kid. Aaron was great at football starting at the age of six. He played football up until his sophomore year in high school. He loved music, he loved video games and he loved sports. Aaron was a family kid, he loved family, he loved for everybody to be together, and he loved friends. He was very close with all of his friends growing up from a little kid into high school. He kept in contact with all of his friends. He was into music. So, he was in the studio just about every weekend trying to do music and get his career started in that area.

Ms. Sasser described the impact of her son's murder by police on his siblings and her emotional well-being, according to the following:

> Just the impact for my daughters, they both took it different. One, she's older and part of her was just [destroyed], she wears his clothes. She takes pictures like he did, and she would put them together. She cries. She's trying to keep him in her. And she likes that same music. She's like, "This is Kenny's favorite. This is it!"

She further stated,

> I know when it's not a good day, whether it's to not come to work or to just keep myself there [work]. I tried therapy really early and it made me angry . . . I kept going over it for a couple of hours and then I just resented [it].

Losing a Friend

Losing a Friend can be understood as the sudden and traumatic death of an individual who shared and influenced relationships with peers. Losing a friend who was suddenly killed by police is a difficult burden to carry for most people. Due to common knowledge that youth relationships have a major influence on their emotional, social, and mental development, experiencing the traumatic murder of a youth by friends presents grave consequences in these areas. Specifically, several participants described experiencing extreme pain, sadness, and hurt following the murder by police of their peer. For example, Kimberly, a friend of a deceased teen, provided the following statement about learning the news of her friend's murder by police:

> So all of a sudden, you know when you on Facebook, they show a news type of report, like somebody was just killed. So I clicked on it, and it said his name, "Kenny Watkins". . . I really just started crying so hard. I couldn't believe it. I call[ed] my granny, "Granny, Kenny gone. They [the police] killed him". It was crazy . . . I think I found out in the middle of the day, almost night time. I really couldn't believe it. I was so sad.

She further acknowledged the impact of her friend's murder on friends and associates in church:

> To know that it was the police that did it, that really hurt me. Our whole church was sad about it, family, friends; he was a known person. A lot of people had respect for him and liked him . . . I don't think he had no enemies.

Losing a friend also disrupts important relationships in the lives of survivors. Specifically, some youth victims possessed girlfriends, and at times a child, in which these individuals are left to carry a major emotional and social burden following the untimely murder of their loved one. For example, a girlfriend of a youth victim provided the following narrative:

> He was my friend before he was my boyfriend. We were real close, I could tell him anything. My best friend . . . not a day went by where I didn't talk to him . . . We phoned every day.

Furthermore, when a teen mother loses her better half to a heinous and unwarranted act of violence by police, her pain and suffering become unbearable. According to Kai, she lost a piece of herself, and in turn, was unable to recover from the emotional and psychological trauma. She stated,

> The day I found out, it's just like a piece of my heart went away. I still feel like I'm not how I used to be before it happened. I can't explain it. That was a real big loss for me, so I'm still trying to get myself together.

Based on the fact that many youth victims were involved in sports and social activities in their school and community, their murder by police also produced emotional and social wounds for the deceased youth's teammates, coaches and teachers, as well as associates who shared these activities. Moreover, many young people are left to find ways to cope with the traumatic death of a friend, which is indicative of the following statement by Precious, mother of a youth killed by police:

> It was just like a ripple effect, with people . . . my heart goes out to them. You'll hear [people say], "I'm praying for you. He was a good dude". . .[Some] kids [got] big tattoos! And I'm like, what are y'all doing? "*King Kenny*" and I'm like, "Whoa!. . ." [They are] just trying to deal with it the best way they can.

Stolen Dreams

Stolen Dreams can be defined as the occurrence when life goals, desires, and aspirations of a youth and his family are suddenly eliminated due to his untimely and traumatic death by police. In other words, the careless act of police murder, primarily in situations where they act as judge and jury, is a major contributor of Black youth's *Stolen Dreams*. For example, several family and friends acknowledged how their deceased loved one's involvement and passion for sports and arts were suddenly shattered following their untimely killing by police. Moreover, some participants believed that youth victims would have become successful and productive young adults, simply due to their gained success and notoriety from peers and adult mentors. For example, Precious acknowledged her son's sports and fashion talents while indicating his possibility for future success, if not for his murder by police:

> Kenny loved fashion and sports, he played football for a long time. His cousin plays college football . . . He looked up to his cousin a lot and I'm sure Kenny could have played college football if he wasn't killed.

Jeremy, a cousin of a deceased youth, added the following about his loved one's *Stolen Dreams*:

> We talked a lot on the phone about college and sports, and he used to look up to me or something like that. He was pretty good [at football] too and I believe he could have made it! I used to give him tips [on] how to stay on track.

Finally, Lakeisha acknowledged how her son's dreams and aspirations to become a successful rap artist and have a big family were disrupted and stolen following his traumatic killing by an off-duty Chicago PD:

> Him (Juice WRLD, hip hop artist) and Aaron were close. They were good friends. He was a good friend to Aaron too. He's doing really good

> in the music industry, so I knew my son would do really good too . . . We all miss that about him because we just thought things would be different. He wanted a big family because he loved football. He told me one day that when he has a family he's going to have a whole football team. At some point I was looking to be a grandmother with a big family. That was taken away, so that's very hurtful! (*It is unfortunate to note that Jarad Higgins, aka Juice WRLD, transitioned on Dec. 8, 2019, Oak Lawn, IL, from a supposed drug overdose. His death occurred five-months following our talk with Ms. Brandon. Details surrounding his untimely death remain suspicious, according to some news outlets.*)

Struggling to Find Justice: Experiences of Discrimination by Courts and Police

Another major theme in this research was family and friends' struggles to find justice following the killing of their loved one by police. Specifically, *Struggling to Find Justice* can be identified as survivors' experiences of discrimination, disrespect, and a lack of empathy or sympathy from police and court officials. These struggles to find justice tend to manifest in different ways, yet are defining moments in the lives of most family and friends of youth killed by police. First, all mothers in this study expressed difficulties gaining access to their child's deceased body in the aftermath of the police killing. Access in this regard can be understood as a mother's ability to observe, identify, validate, and be with her child's body following the sudden and traumatic death by police. In addition, several mothers were denied access to their child at the crime scene and morgue by police and other law enforcement officials who were present. They were further denied the opportunity to identify and validate their son's killing by police. For example, Precious provided the following narrative:

> I feel that they just thought I was some regular Black woman that walked the street, I have no clue. He says, oh well, according to HIPAA law we can't give you [Kenny]. . . I say, okay, I'm very understanding. So I asserted my professionalism. I understand the HIPAA law. However,. . . they're trying to find out his age. Because he looked really young, he just made 18 in May [2019].

Furthermore, Ms. Nicole expressed being denied access by police at the morgue to view and identify her son's deceased body for *four days*, according to the following:

> When I finally went to see Corshawn, the police wouldn't let me see my son for four days. They told me to go to the morgue the next day, day after day, after day. He [is] not ready, he not ready, he not ready, he not ready.

The next phase of struggling to find justice included family and friends' experiences of discrimination and disrespect during court hearings. For example, several loved ones of youth victims expressed feeling disrespected, unheard, and invalidated by judges and DAs during court hearings. Specifically, Precious acknowledged being invalidated by the courts after spending 11 days during the trial, only to be informed that ***she did not prove*** to be the mother of the deceased youth victim, based on the following:

> The judge said they were supposed to put me on the stand just to acknowledge (me). But the judge initially said that I didn't have to go on the stand unless the case went to the second round. I would have to talk about my emotions. So I sat in court for 11 days for them to tell me that I wasn't his [Kenny Watkins, teen killed by police] mother. That it hadn't been proven that I was his mother. That's just the minimum of all the stuff that went on.

She further acknowledged being disrespected and intimidated during the court proceeding by the officer who killed her son and his colleagues:

> I informed them that he (the officer who killed her son) was staring at me in court, the officer. When I (went) to the restroom, there was this black guy that was sitting there and he said, "Is that your guy?" And he said other racist negativity . . . There was a black woman passing and I said, "No, that's the man that brought up my son." He was like, "Oh". He would stare at me and make eye contact, I had some reason to be afraid . . . Whether I walk out first or he walks out first and there was never an acknowledgment from her [the judge]. She read from this book and that was that.

Cassina, aunt of teen murdered by police, further expressed sentiments of being disrespected and discriminated against by the judge during the court proceeding:

> Goes through the whole ordeal and then she told Precious that she couldn't cry. She told us no emotions, no crying . . . in court. She told us that . . . I am not exaggerating this. You mean to tell me, you just showed me a picture of Kenny in a position that I don't want to see him in ever and you're going to tell me I can't have a facial expression behind that? What are you talking about? If this was your white pilgrim sitting up there, you'd do it [cry and show emotions] too. That whole procedure was just a circus. It was a joke. They only did it to pacify us, making it seem like we wanted money.

Devaluing and Dehumanizing Black Life by Police

Another major theme that emerged was the *Devaluing of Black Life by Police*. On several instances, family and friends alluded to the idea of why and how their youth loved one was killed by police. Their question was based on experiences and an understanding of youth victims as loving and caring human beings, and they were unsure how police could justify murdering a youth, especially those killed in broad daylight. Many family and friends carry regret of wishing their loved one was not at the *Wrong Place at the Wrong Time* and believed that police lacked remorse for taking their lives. Moreover, lack of police accountability in the aftermath of youth victims' death only adds "fuel to the fire." For example, Kimberly, a close friend of a teen victim, shared the following:

> It's crazy. It's like I wish he wasn't there. I wish this didn't happen to him . . . The police don't regret it. They're not sorry. And 9 times out of 10, when you hear the news about the police killing somebody, and a Black person at that, it's either they get a slap on the wrist, they get fired or they get suspended, and then they're back working again.

Furthermore, Kia, girlfriend of deceased teen victim, shared the following regarding police devaluing and criminalizing Black lives and in turn, fueling Black people's distrust toward police:

> I feel his (Corshawn, teen killed by police) frustration, so he probably would go out and . . . you know, I don't know. That's because y'all treat him like he's a criminal. Just because he has dreads, or just because this, that, and the third. We all are human. So that's why I feel like people don't like the police because they don't care about us, really. And sometimes they over-do their job. Y'all [police] are supposed to protect us, not put us [in] harm's way.

Police Cover-ups

Police Cover-ups was a major subtheme related to the devaluing of Black lives by police. *Police Cover-ups* can be defined as the system's (police, judges, courts, etc.) attempt to protect police from unlawful practices and wrongdoing following a youth murder by police. As noted in Chapter 2, the law enforcement bill of rights, or LEOBOR provisions and contracts, act as a constitution to protect and privilege police during accusations of criminal abuse, misconduct, and police killings (Havorlson, 2022). These attempts are further intended to criminalize the victim via the media (news and social media outlets), with hopes that the general public will find the officers' behaviors and actions *JUSTIFIED*. For example, several days after her son was killed by cops, Ms. Nicole learned that her son was followed and brutalized by officers two days before they killed him. This act of brutality left deep welt marks on her son's body that were visible to the eye; however, out of fear and terror, her son refused to reveal the source of his pain and injuries, but a friend extended the information. Ms. Nicole stated,

> He [Corshawn, her son] stayed in the house, but the police had jumped on him. May 28th (2017), five days before they killed him . . . I didn't know until after he passed away, when some of his friends showed me text messages and things. He was actually texting them when they were following him, and they [police] broke his phone.

Despite a mother's concern and observation of major injuries to her son's body, the irony is that these same welt marks were "removed" or absent from her son's body when she identified him at the morgue. As a result, police cover-ups occurred in this regard as a possible attempt to remove important evidence of police brutality and unlawful practices experienced by the deceased youth. Ms. Nicole noted,

> Nothing. Those scratches . . . When I pulled that blue cover off of him, those scratches were gone. It was a big green patch, they were gone. Do you hear me?. . . I just got chills. Gone. Yes, disappeared. They must've did something. My belief is maybe that was the DNA from five days before, when they must've grabbed him, scratched him, or whatever. They was gone. I took some pictures of [his] arm.

Furthermore, police cover-ups seem to be a primary reason why young people, especially those residing in urban settings, distrust and dislike the police. Police cover-ups, in the form of lies and falsifying information, are reflections of police abuse of power and authority, as well as justification for police use of lethal force. For example, Kai stated that "People don't like the police because they [are] not doing their job. They just do what they want to do, basically. I feel like they take that authority over their head." She went on to suggest,

> Laquan McDonald, he just now got justice and it happened so long ago.
>
> And, it's like they try to cover up, and that's not right . . . that don't make no sense. And how do you [police] even sleep at night knowing that you did this? Then you come up with lies, and this is a whole human being [teen victim]. You come up with lies about what they did to make you kill them. No!

Finally, dehumanizing the victim and his community is also part of police cover-ups. Specifically, fault is placed on the victim's environment by the media for the police use of violence. For example, Dr. Stovall reflected on the case of Rekia Boyd's murder by an off-duty Chicago PD officer. In this case, Officer Servin attempted to justify his actions due to a noise disturbance and Black youth gathering at a party. Moreover, officers at the crime scene ran background checks on several teens at the party in an attempt to criminalize the victim and party attendees, as well as to *JUSTIFY* their use of violence. In sum, these police tactics were intended to place fault on the victim for her own death, prior to a thorough investigation of the circumstances that led to a Black youth's homicide by police. Dr. Stovall believed that these police practices are based on deeply rooted anti-Black sentiments. He provided the following:

> So the fault is still on the people, this thing around, if you weren't so violent, if you weren't so prone to engage in this way, we wouldn't have these problems. Missing from the whole narratives, no, you came out of your house, you left your house. And not in proximity to your house. You left your house from a distance, to approach a group of young folks, because the common assumption is that they're up to something . . . At one point they were try[ing] to do all these background checks on folks who were witnesses . . . to the police, to discredit them. So they were all criminals anyway [to police]. This type of rationale [is] rooted in deeply racist sentiment . . . anti-black sentiment against particular community members, and a long history of trying to discredit folks for something that was at no point in time, their fault.

Family and Community as Anchors of Support

Several family and friends of youth killed by police acknowledged *Family and Community as Anchors of Support*. Specifically, *family* can be defined as people who live in close proximity and experience similar struggles with the intent to support, provide, and protect each other. Family, in this regard, runs deeper than blood, but is based on mutually shared support and Love amidst everyday trials and struggles. For example, Precious, mother of a teen murdered by LAPD, expressed the following: "So it's hard for me to try to understand, it was always just me and my kids. His father, their father has been here and talking to him helps." Family tends to act as a direct source of care and comradery following a youth killing by police. Each family member holds a unique relationship with the deceased, in which a youth's untimely murder by police can create emotional and psychological trauma for the family, further influencing their need and desire to support each other. For example, Jeremy, cousin of teen killed by police, noted the following:

> I was making sure Precious was okay . . . That's my thought process . . . to reach out to her, and make sure she's okay, because . . . it's [her] son who lost his life . . . We spoke about it as a family. I'm really close with my cousin, Lonny [pseudonym]. We talked about it. Lonny is Kenny's uncle. We spoke about it.

In addition, community members and resources may also act as an *Anchor of Support* for family and friends of youth killed by police. Specifically, Ms. Nicole discussed receiving support from a women's group known as *The Unwanted Sorority* and *Mothers of Black Boys (MOBB). The Unwanted Sorority*, originally founded by Eric Russell, is a community of parents who lost a child to police violence. Furthermore, *MOBB* is an inspirational support group for Black mothers who lost a son to violence, to acknowledge the positive characteristics of their child's legacy. Ms. Nicole described these groups as important and meaningful forms of support in her life currently and shortly after her son's killing by police. She believes that the Unwanted Sorority and MOBB act as vital resources for her and other parents due to the fact that all members can relate and understand the lived pain and hardships endured after losing a child to police violence. Ms. Nicole stated,

> Eric Russell, he really has helped me. Ah! That is my brother. Yes! So, I have them [support groups]. They keep me pumped up [and] going. It's a group of women that Eric started. We're called the *Unwanted Sorority*. . . . That's mothers, or dads. Parents, but mostly women, who have lost their children to police brutality. So we're like the ones they don't want to see coming! That's why we're called the Unwanted Sorority . . . I have only met one of them, but the closeness of that, we talk on the phone [and] social media. You're not alone in that group at all.

She went on to suggest,

> M-O-B-B, stands for *MOBB* . . . *Mothers of Black Boys*. . . Because it talks about mothers, where you put out good stuff about your kids graduating or they're doing something. Then, it's really a support group for

the moms. You're not alone with this [group]. And then, you can't talk to everybody about this or they'll be like, "I feel you.". . . So this is a group where women are like, "No, you did your best. We all go through things." I love that. I love them.

Holding Police Accountable

Another important theme in this work was *Holding Police Accountable*. This theme has been continuously depicted as a major issue of policing during this study and a prior one. According to youth victims' family and friends, the root of holding police accountable is based on the victim as undeserving of his untimely murder by police, and rather than being punished, officers are rewarded with an administrative 30-day leave, or paid time off. The problem with such an outcome is simple: The victim rarely receives justice and the police perpetrator is rarely, if ever, prosecuted and held accountable for the loss of life. Havorlson (2022) would argue that this type of privilege for police during a criminal investigation is due to law enforcement officers' bill of rights (LEOBORs) provisions, which he argues are primary causes of police lack of accountability following a police-involved homicide. Most interviewees believed that police should be charged and convicted of killings as would be the case for most if not all people. For example, Kai provided the following statement:

People don't deserve that (murdered by police) at all. Then it's another thing for

somebody else to kill them (police) and you can get justice, but it's another thing where the police do it and [they] try to give you a settlement (i.e., Money as Justice) and you're just supposed to be okay with it. Y'all humans just like we are. If y'all do a crime, y'all supposed to be held accountable for it, period.

She goes on to suggest,

The police only get 30 days leave. They bleed just like us. So, why do they get to kill

people and then it's just fear for them where they only get a 30 day leave. Why don't they get jail time?. . . Who is that help[ing]? Dead people?! There's people out here going through depression like me and she (interviewee's daughter) [is] never going to meet her dad. Ever, ever, ever. It just don't make no sense.

Ms. Brandon, mother of deceased teen, added the following:

> I think they need to be charged just like they would charge a regular citizen with whatever crime that they're doing. If they were wrong, they need to be held accountable by being charged criminally like they would do a regular citizen. They shouldn't get a slap on the wrist like they get. They need to be criminally charged.

Transforming Trauma Into Activism: Family as Activists

It is no coincidence that following a parent's or family member's experience of trauma and her search for justice following a child's murder by police, it is clear how these events can transform trauma into activism, or a family member into an activist. *Transforming trauma into activism* can be described as an unexpected and traumatic occurrence that has a direct influence on the positionality and involvement of an individual. Thus, the traumatic event moves the individual to search for justice in the aftermath, which in turn can lead to the individual's involvement in activism and organizing. In other words, the parent who becomes an activist may not consciously choose this positionality, but lived trauma and suffering, as well as the search for answers to what and why her child was killed by police, are primary contributors to this journey. According to Mr. Montes, a parent will embrace the fight at all cost, despite the struggle, with hopes of receiving justice for their child. For example, he described the following:

> After two and half years, the mother said, "You know what? We're tired of this!" We've had vigils or masses every year on the anniversary of his killing. They have something for his birthday and we go to mass and they say his name. And they've also become involved in our other activities to fight Trump campaigns, our May Day march and rally . . . We stop and lower the lift and then the family gets up there and they denounce the police killers, in Spanish and English.

In addition, Mr. Russell discussed the experiences of galvanizing 100 mothers nationwide who lost a child to police violence. The group attended a day of action on Capitol Hill (Washington D.C.) to demand police transparency and accountability for their deceased youth. He suggested,

> As a community we need to galvanize in a real sort of way to advocate for police reform, transparency, and accountability. I was absolutely shocked

last March [2019]. I took a hundred mothers to Washington D.C. for a day of action to address members of the Congressional Black Congress. And when I got on Capitol Hill, I was pulled over in some room and questioned by Capitol Hill security, Jeff Sessions, and Donald Trump had put me on an extreme Black identity activist list.

Findings: Community Members (Activists, Reporters, Lawyers, and Neighbors)

Contextualizing Police Violence in Low-Income Black and Brown Communities

When considering the impact of police killings of youth on community members and activists, *Contextualizing Police Violence in Low-Income Black and Brown Communities* was a major theme that evolved. Specifically, several individuals discussed the historical etiology of extrajudicial killings in these communities. Moreover, due to assumed high rates of Black and Brown impoverished residents, and in turn high crime, interviewees acknowledged that policing in these communities has historically been grounded in practices of violence, unlawfulness, and at times, murder. In other words, police killings of youth in low-income Black and Brown communities currently remain part of a long-standing tradition of police oppression and brutality in the United States. For example, Dr. Stovall, college professor and community activist in Chicago, provided a historical example of state-sanctioned violence by police toward the Black Community in Chicago. Specifically, he discussed the supposed *Urban Legend*, which was later revealed to be true by "reporters from the *London Guardian*" (Ackerman, 2015), surrounding the police torture site of Blacks at *Homan Square*. David stated that during his upbringing, he learned that Black people were arrested and taken to Homan Square without being processed and later tortured by police. He provided the following:

> A story I think is important is one of Homan Square and (it) isn't necessarily a space around police killing, but it was essentially a space where [police] was conducting torture on suspects. So these weren't people who were convicted of anything. Right? They were taken in holding and actually not processed, but tortured. And as a Southsider [of Chicago]. . . there's often this thing as a young person growing up about the urban legends of both places. Our friends would say, "Look, you don't want to get caught up by the cops out West because they might take you and just detain you indefinitely."

He further suggested,

> A group of reporters from the London Guardian figured out that was actually true. So this was literally a space where you could be detained indefinitely and anything could happen in your detainment. So this thing around understanding that [police torture] as normalized practice becomes important. So where it's not connected as much to police shootings and deaths, it's connected to state sanctioned violence in the form of law enforcement.

Eric Russell, community activist in Chicago, also provided evidence surrounding historical racialized violence and discrimination by Chicago police and White citizenry toward Black residents. According to Mr. Russell's narrative, these examples can be further understood as racist Deputized Violence by vigilantes that was sanctioned by the State. He stated,

> First of all, it's a racist community (Chicago PD). The Chicago police have a long history. They used to arrest Black gang members and drop them off in White communities so the White gang members would beat them up and they would have to get back to their hood. But the likelihood of a Black kid getting back to the ghetto, having to navigate a white community and not being assaulted was very low. So that was the punishment from the police. They [police] will question you, violate your Civil Rights, and then they'll take you to the White community and say, "Now you get back home." And most brothers end up being (assaulted) by White boys on the way home.

Finally, Pharoah Mitchell, community activist in Antelope Valley, CA (near LA), provided the following statement related to historical violence and brutality by LA Sheriffs toward Section 8 housing (low-income) Black and Brown residents. His depiction is reflective of Kraska's (2007) argument regarding militarization of policing in relation to the SWAT teams' raid, search, and seizure of residents for menial drug accusations. Mr. Mitchell suggested the following:

> The law firms cite racism in Section 8 policing. So it wasn't only X Sheriff's Department, it was the Sheriff's Department involved too with raids! They came 15 deep in people's houses. One lady refused to let them in the house, they literally climbed through her window and left footprints on her dresser climbing in her window. They kept finding the same *phantom weed*, it was a roach, maybe about this size (hold fingers about one inch apart), a little bit longer, that they kept finding in people's houses. And they would go as bold as saying, "Hey, bitch or nigger, we'll plant this weed in your house ain't nothing that you can do." And they kept finding the phantom weed!

FIGURE 4.2 Corner of Wabash Street and 58 Street in Chicago, IL where a youth victim was killed by police.

Police Terrorism as a Form of Structural Violence

Police Terrorism as a Form of Structural Violence was also an important theme that evolved from community members' and activists' narratives. *Structural Violence* can be defined as a system of political and economic rules, laws, and sanctions that create and maintain harmful living conditions for an individual, community, or group (Outland, 2019, p. 244). Structural in the sense that politics and laws prevent residents' access to necessary resources (i.e., Food, clothing, shelter, gainful employment, and support services) to control and determine their own lives. Violent in the sense that these conditions usually lead to harmful, and at times deadly, outcomes for residents. *Police terrorism acts as a form of Structural Violence* when officers patrol certain areas or citizenry in unlawful, violent, and destructive ways. Police terrorism further acts as a form of structural violence due to police receiving protection and justification by the system following the untimely murder of a youth. In this research, police terrorism as a form of Structural Violence manifested in two important ways, including *Predictive Policing, or Operation LASER*, and *Housing, Education, and Employment Discrimination.*

Predictive Policing: Operation LASER

What is *predictive policing*? According to Ms. Garcia, community activist and nurse in LA, predictive policing can be defined as the identification and surveillance of persons of interest based on criminal suspicion using advanced technology and increased law enforcement. In other words, criminal profiles of individuals or communities are developed using advanced technological surveillance systems (Bhuiyan, 2021).

Project "Operation LASER" marked the launch of predictive policing in South LA. According to Jamie, this project was intended to track chronic offenders in South LA using advanced technological identification and surveillance systems. Such systems included, but were not limited to, the use of drone devices, chronic offender bulletins, and community zoning according to the level of crime. Thus, the overall aim of operation LASER was to legitimize police violence and increase law enforcement in different locales of South LA, which are major dangers, according to Jamie:

> So that becomes part and parcel of this kind of reengineering of policing, which has two folds where it's not anything new. Because if you talk to people, it's the same violent policing it's always been. But the danger is that, now that they have technology behind them, their ability to collect data, repurpose it, reconstruct it, in order to legitimize and deem you criminal and worthy of being murdered, incarcerated, [and] displaced, is like triplefold. And so that's the big danger of where and how it's changed.

A major component of Operation LASER is the practice of *Zoning* in South LA urban communities. According to Ms. Garcia, Zoning consists of utilizing a chronic offender bulletin by LAPD based on the level of crime in a given area. These chronic offender bulletins are used by LAPD to create a criminal identification profile of a "person of interest." As a result, additional law enforcement officers occupy and patrol communities deemed as high-crime areas, and they are more likely to use violence and lethal force during random stop and search of assumed criminal suspects. Jamie suggested that "so through automatic license plate readers, through CCTVs (closed-circuit television cameras), through the field interview card and stopping them. Looking for them [profiled criminal suspects] in different areas that they have demarcated as being crime-ridden areas."

Furthermore, in criminology and criminal justice research and evidence-based practices, predictive policing practices such as Operation LASER are known as *hotspot policing*. Law enforcement agencies use these practices to oversaturate Black, Brown, and low-income neighborhoods with an extensive number of police officers and gang and crime units to violently curtail and eliminate targets (i.e., criminals) they deem dangerous and violent within these communities. Moreover, the exuberant amount of public tax dollars and resources paid to support police overtime are used to fund these initiatives and programs, which *claim* to reduce crime in these communities. However, a thorough review of crime statistics in these communities reveals not only a lack of crime reduction but rather consistent crime patterns, and in some cases, an increase in crime in these communities.

According to Ms. Garcia, Kenny Watkins's murder by LA police, along with six other young Black and Brown teen males, was a result of Operation LASER and Zoning predictive police practices. Specifically, and as previously noted, Zones identified as high-crime areas are granted extensive levels of enforcement and officers patrolling these areas are more likely to use violence and lethal force. Thus, on the day of Kenny's murder, the area of South LA near Figueroa was deemed as a high-crime area. Moreover, according to the chronic bulletin report, a Black male, in his 30s, and armed, was identified as a criminal suspect. Although Kenny did not fit the profile of said suspect, he and other urban teen males became victims of predictive policing and Zoning police practices due to *being in the wrong place at the wrong time* (e.g., Kenny was gunned down while riding his bike by an officer who shot several times from his patrol car; i.e., drive-by shooting). In other words, Kenny's untimely death was not an accident, but a by-product of Operation LASER and person-based predictive policing, referred to as *hot-spot* policing by law enforcement. Jamie concluded with the following: "And so I was going back through some research last night, again in preparing for this, and he was one of six youth that were killed that year between the ages of 14 and 18 years old."

Housing and Race Discrimination

Housing and Race Discrimination were also forms of structural violence that evolved from the narratives of community members and activists. Specifically, several participants acknowledged that simply being a resident in low-income housing and a person of Color can lead to becoming a target of police terrorism and violence. In such cases, police and White community members are granted authority by government officials to violate and abuse poor Black and Brown citizens. In this regard, this form of discrimination can be understood as Deputized Violence, in which the local governance body permits and encourages state-sanctioned (police) and racialized vigilante (White community members) violence against minority bodies. For example, Mr. Smith makes the connection between housing and race discrimination and state-sanctioned violence by police, according to the following:

> People of low economic status, they would get a voucher and they apply to what's available through the federal government. Out here, the district is predominantly White and in [Lancaster] and the city of Palmdale, they were the city power structure. The Los Angeles County Sheriff's department was pretty much just pro-racially profiling African Americans and Latinos, anybody who was on Section 8. At that time, [the sheriff] sent out a decree that created this commission called the Section 8 Commission and [gave] this commission the authority to literally do what Trump is doing . . ."people need to go back to where they came from, Section 8 is not wanted here."

In addition, Eric highlighted unlawful practices and abuses by banks and money lenders toward low-income housing residents in Chicago, according to the following:

> And the horror of the hunt. Chicago, in many ways, is the epicenter of our pitiful struggle. We talk about what it is. Although we have so much ugliness . . . death is an ugly thing. For me, I don't fear death, because how I started out, I started out protecting the land. I helped spearhead the class action lawsuits against Bank of America, Countrywide, IndyMac, and Household Finance for predatory lending, red lining, and institutional racism . . . . They were stealing Black people's houses.

Finally, Mr. Mitchell added how those residents who reside in Section 8 housing became primary targets of state-sanctioned and deputized violence by LA Sheriffs and community members. These campaigns of organized terror were not limited to the homes of residents, but extended to social media outlets, according to the following:

> They [local White neighbors] scrawled on Michele's door. The neighbors were throwing piss. Her children were on their way to school. The harassment that they got with big swastikas and things like that in people's front yards . . . Intimidating people on Section 8 to stop coming up there. And it was mainly done by Rex Parris.
>
> (Note: Rex Parris is the current Mayor of Lancaster, LA County, *Cityoflancasterca.org, 2024)*

He further added,

> Right here (while pointing at an old Antelope Valley News Article) it says, "We hate Section 8. Fuck them niggers". . . on the social media, they literally put up a Website, "I Hate Section 8". . . And that's a picture of the "We Hate Section 8" signs.
>
> *(Daily Journal, 2012)*

This account provided by Mr. Mitchell was also echoed by Mr. Smith's account of housing and racial discrimination and Deputized Violence. He stated,

> They'd put a swastika on the garage, they'd urinated in the lawn, they'd dropped feces . . . one person threw urine on the mom's son. All of this was going on and the Los Angeles County Sheriff's Department, along with the Housing Department, along with the city officials, all were funding these officers to literally raid these homes of people who identified as Section 8.

Impact of Activism on the Activists

Impact of Activism on the Activists was another important theme that was denoted in this research. Specifically, although all activists appeared committed in their stance against police terrorism and discrimination toward predominantly low-income Black and Brown communities, they also acknowledged the adverse impact activism can have on the activists. For instance, Mr. Smith, community activist in Palmdale, CA, expressed the following sentiments about his fear of being shot as an activist:

> At this point, we're (African Americans) about 14% of the population, from '94 up to now, it's still a significant part of the population from our communities that don't trust the L.A. County Sheriff's Department . . . no matter what we're trying to do to try to break down that wall, the goal is to try to work towards peace, but there's still that fear that you'll be shot!

He further acknowledged experiences of family challenges coupled with psychological stress resulting from activism, based on the following:

> It's stressful. The impact is quite stressful because I take this home. I don't get paid for what I'm doing. Having to talk to families about someone

> being beaten up by the Sheriff's Department when I'm trying to make every effort to try to make things work out here in a peaceful environment is quite unbearable, to be honest with you. Because I've got a family myself. I've got two daughters and my wife and they want to know why I spend so much time fighting for [others].

In addition, Mr. Mitchell discussed some of the adverse impacts activism had on his life. Specifically, he spoke of the dangers of activism, in which his life and family members have been threatened on occasions. Pharaoh stated,

> Even through the stuff that we've done, the death calls [and] death threats that we've gotten. I've literally [been] at my daughter's school . . . and they're (LA sheriffs) literally driving . . . I've got my truck in the dirt, they're literally driving up in the dirt and driving back.

Mr. Russell also discussed experiences of receiving death threats from community members and being intimidated and harassed by Chicago PD:

> Just the other day . . . I have two German Shepherds, and I have social media . . . Some lady called me the other day and said that she hoped that my dogs rip my throat out at night and I won't be able to speak. You know, I get stuff like that. The police, they follow me from crime scenes and trot me with their lights and flash their lights on me and pull me over for different things. Like when I come to crime scenes, if I'm not parked properly, I come back to my car and I have a bunch of tickets. You know, in a crime scene, cars are everywhere.

Coping With Trauma

In addition, *Coping With Trauma* following the untimely murder of a youth killed by police can also have an adverse impact on the family and friends, according to activists and community members. For example, Carlos discussed many parents, as well as siblings, of deceased young people who continuously struggle with trauma. These struggles can have a grave impact on a family member's ability to function during daily life, which in turn can cause disruptions in one's academic, professional, and social functioning. This finding aligns with those of Outland and Colleagues' (2020) study, in which they validated symptoms of complex trauma vis-à-vis the survivors' narratives and stories of youth killed by police. For example, Carlos describes the experience of a family's struggle with trauma after their loved one was murdered by police:

> Talking to the mom, the dad, the sister, the brothers, just trauma, heavy trauma, and how to deal with the trauma. I mean the lawyer recommended counseling and they went to counseling, but talk to the mom Josefina . . . . Josefina Liso is his mom and Juan Mendez is the dad. He said they went for six months but it doesn't help, trauma is trauma.

Mr. Montes describes the economic and social impact of trauma on parents following their child's murder by police, which in turn carries the potential to destroy and erode the family unit:

> Jesse Romero's dad's name is Jesse Romero Sr. and the mom is Teresa Dominguez. Working class, Spanish speaking . . . They got evicted, they moved out [due to] trauma. He had a younger brother named Richard . . . that (Jesse's death) really traumatized him a lot. He dropped out of school. He wouldn't agree to go to counseling and then he started getting arrested and harassed. But my main point was what? That it tore the family apart.

Furthermore, Zak Koeske, critical reporter for the *Chicago Times*, noted that after several phone meetings with Aaron Brandon's mother and girlfriend, he concluded that the teen male's loved ones were deeply impacted by the loss. Moreover, he suggested that he struggled to understand "how" the young man's mother and girlfriend were able to move on following Mr. Brandon's untimely death, as well as another past tragedy that struck this family deeply, which are suggestive of the following:

> Another thing that really struck me at the time was after I spoke with the girlfriend who was only 15 or 16 years old, she was obviously very emotional. And then we had to end our interview because she had to go to work, because she was working at a burger joint. To think that (she) had to deal with that kind of loss, and then go to work and serve people hamburgers or whatever a few hours later, seemed really tragic.

He went on to suggest,

> I would communicate off and on with both his girlfriend and mother. I never met the mother, but spoke with her on the phone once or twice,

and communicated, I want to say, maybe once via email, and I communicated via email with the girlfriend. One of the things that I learned was that I covered a situation, it wasn't police-related, a year prior where Aaron Brandon's father and two of his sisters were killed in [what] the police described as some sort of targeted hit where they [shooters], in the middle of the night, broke into the family's home and killed the sisters, who were then like 10 and three years old (Reference for Brandon's father and sisters death; Shaw, 2021).

Struggle for Justice: Community Organizing as Tool to Fight Police Violence in Low-Income Black and Brown Communities

Many activists and community members acknowledged the importance of community organizing during their struggle to receive Justice following a youth murder by police. *Community Organizing* can be deemed as being actively engaged in identifying allies and creating a collective voice and stand against forms of structural violence, including police terrorism and unlawful practices. Activists and community members believed and provided evidence that when the community is willing to organize and struggle for Justice following the police killing of a youth, then chances of gaining Justice for victims and their families are inevitable. For example, Carlos Montes, LA community activist, discussed current and past experiences organizing with the Mexican and Chicano community against education and police discrimination, which is reflected in the following statement:

> Well, we have to fight. We have to unite and fight back. We have to, and if we fight, we will win. That's a kind of cliché nowadays, if we fight we win, but it's true . . . . We fought against the charter schools, and we won. We got the Chief back, he retired early and Baka was prosecuted, and we exposed [corruption].

He further suggested,

> For us as a community, we don't do nothing, but this time, we proved that Chicanos or the Mexicans were fighting back. We didn't take it lying down, we protested. We had a big protest in front of LAPD headquarters during the spring. Five-hundred students and families [were] there, and we blasted them [voices of attendees], and the media covered it . . . So I would say unite, and fight.

In addition, Jamie Garcia, activist for *Stop Police Spying Coalition of LA*, denoted the importance of being part of a diverse coalition of community members with goals of bringing together collective minds and ideas to address police terrorism and abuse. She suggested,

> It's a wide range and diverse group of people and I think it allows us to kind of enter into looking at predictive policing from these multiple levels where we are learning how to be allies, learning how to partner with communities in effective ways but then also learning how to take direction. For example, we are attempting to get an op-ed published which we're finding a lot of difficulties because the way that we see things is often not for the public . . . The public doesn't necessarily want to consume an abolitionist perspective on policing. For example, we came up with the idea in the group meeting, right, everybody's together and then a few of us took that on and we took it on and we wrote. Then we're getting input from each other, collectively writing this op-ed, which is a challenge in itself to collectively do something together, bring ideas together.

Finally, Mr. Smith discussed experiences organizing with the *Community Advisory Council (CAC)* and local allies to fight against LA Sheriffs' wrongful abuses of Section 8 housing residents. Due to CAC's efforts and other legal advocacy groups in Palmdale, including *Neighborhood Legal Services*, they sued the LA County sheriff's department and the city of Palmdale for unlawful practices and abuses. According to Jesse, these practices included, but not limited to, harsh jail sentences and racial discrimination against African Americans and Latinos, sheriff harassment and unlawful raids of Section 8 housing residents, which are denoted in the following statements: "African Americans, Latinos seem to get the harsh [jail sentences], arrest, [and] the prosecution! And we get felonies that stick and we don't get them off." Furthermore, CAC won several lawsuits that ended in court settlements and as a result, "they (city of Palmdale) agreed to no longer fund the sheriff's department." Moreover, this struggle was a major victory, or a form of *Reparation*, for African American and Latino residents in Palmdale, CA, according to the following:

> The people who actually were violated . . . meaning their vouchers were taken or if the county sheriff unjustly racially profiled them, arrested them, put them in the back of the Paddy wagon, had them in jail for a significant amount of time . . . they actually got money back, a number of them got thousands of thousands back. So we actually won a victory, I think we [received] $2.1 billion. Now that technically was our 40 acres and a mule.

Jesse believes in the importance of community activism and not accommodating the power structure, as well as when community members are willing to fight, the chance to win is inevitable. These types of struggles, according to Mr. Smith, are foundational to ending police violence, discrimination, and brutality of low-income Black and Brown residents, based on the following:

> [They] just wanted to accommodate the power structure . . . be nice. But, I come from [a place] when we see injustice, we get out there and we fight! So I was the first one to get out with a bullhorn and wait in front of City Hall and tell them, "This is unacceptable!" And as that began to take place, then there were other brothers that came and said "talk to you later." They came around, Foundational, Nation of Islam, Muhammad, all of us got together and said enough is enough! And that was one of the reasons why we got . . .138 rules that were implemented in the city of Lancaster and Palmdale on what the police can and cannot do. We changed the section of laws so that they could no longer racially profile African Americans.

Meaning of Activism: Exposing Systems of Structural Violence

Meaning of Activism, or what it means to be an activist, was a final theme highlighted by community members and activists. Specifically, being an activist primarily involves exposing systems of structural violence against marginalized victims (e.g., police murder and violence). In other words, activism entails being part of the struggle for justice for oppressed communities. Furthermore, being an activist means speaking truth to power, or Giving Voice to the Voiceless. If one has a voice or a platform, several activists and community members believe that this tool could be useful to address state-sanctioned violence and abuse by police. For instance, Ms. Garcia made the following connection between what it means to be an activist and the fight against predictive policing:

> So kind of going back to our timeline, right after we filed the lawsuit in February 2018, we released the report called *Before the Bullet Hits the Body (Stop LAPD Spying, 2018)*. And in that report . . . And it's called *Dismantling Predictive Policing in Los Angeles.* So Before the Bullet Hits the Body: Predictive Policing in Los Angeles. Part of what the work that the *Stop LAPD Spying Coalition* does is really reorienting or adding to the fight, where we react, and we take to the streets, and we demand that this is not acceptable. And there's this indignation, like this has to stop!

She further stated,

> Then there's this other fight that says we're going to expose the systems that create the conditions of murder and violence in our communities.

> So, during that time, as we were getting more documents from the initial lawsuits that we filed in February 2018, we were able to obtain some reports about Operation LASER.

In addition, Mr. Henderson, critical lawyer in Chicago, discussed the meaning of his work in regard to speaking truth to power in the courtroom, according to the following:

> And I think people want lawyers, as I mentioned, Judge Montgomery, who will stand up and speak truth to power. David and Goliath, that's what motivates me. And so I'm motivated and I just keep believing that if we stay at it and do it in a public way, we have the press walls and we hold press conferences. You walked in the hallway, you saw some of the articles. Let's shine a light on it.

Furthermore, Mr. Russell discussed his activism and utilizing it to support and fight for justice for families who were impacted by police violence. He stated,

> Well, any time there's a police-involved shooting, people call me. People call me because they're familiar with my stance and with my boots on the ground and over the years I've taken a lot of families down to the police board to do victim impact statements as advocate, as spokesman, for various families. Even when it comes to the consent decree, *the Tree of Life Justice League*, I provided the plaintiffs for the class action lawsuit. Before the consent decree, we sued the police.

Finally, Mr. Koeske discussed the importance of his reporting in providing *Voice to the Voiceless*. He believed that reporting can be a useful tool to demonstrate genuine care and concern to marginalized groups as well as disseminating their true story to the public, based on the following:

> I would just say that as a reporter, I am interested in telling your family's story, your loved one's story, and trying to understand who they were, and what happened to them in this situation. Regardless of what I end up finding, I'm interested in learning more about them, and like I said, I value anyone and showing them that someone does care, and that I'm not just going through the motions, or I'm not necessarily accepting the police narrative of events, and that there is somebody who is going to listen to them. Even if I'm doing so in the capacity of my profession, I'm still there, and I'm happy to listen, and try to empathize.

FIGURE 4.3 Visualization of "The Ripple Effect."

Summation of Findings, The Ripple Effect: Impact of Youth Killings by Police on Families and Communities

In order to make sense of the epidemic of state-sanctioned violence, or police terrorism, of Black and Brown low-income communities, it is necessary to perceive this impact from a holistic lens. Holistic in the sense that the impact of police terrorism on the friends, family, and community members of the deceased youth must be strongly considered. This holistic impact can be deemed as *The Ripple Effect. The Ripple Effect* occurs when a youth is untimely murdered by police, and the trauma, pain, and suffering related to this sudden death spreads and takes root in the hearts, minds, and lives of those who Loved, respected, and cared for the deceased youth. In other words, it is rare that the family and community of a youth killed by police can escape the impact of the Ripple Effect. In addition, according to the frequency of Black and Brown citizens who are murdered by police, this experience can be deemed as *Becoming Part of a Larger Trauma Story*. Furthermore, not only are Black, Brown, and Poor people frequently killed by police in the United States, but it is also common knowledge that most officers are rarely, if ever, held accountable for these deceased human beings. In other words, police actions that led to the youth's death are all too frequently deemed *JUSTIFIED* by the judicial system. Thus, the officer who killed a youth is granted a pass by the system to return to active duty to patrol the same community where the deceased youth resided; thus, furthering the experiences of police terrorism and fear of traumatized residents. In closing, for Black people in the United States, a major challenge with becoming part of this story is its ***unpredictability***, which is reflected in Ms. Turner's statement:

> When I pulled up at the location (crime scene of Kenny's murder by police), it was just [yellow] tape and news media. And the first thing I thought was "damn, we're [on] this side of the tape now." Like we're that story now. Like you see the stories all the time and it doesn't bother you really. It hurts because it's a Black person. It hurts because you see a mother crying, but you don't really understand her cry. You don't understand the grief that somebody that is in this world to protect you just took somebody from you.

References

Ackerman, S. (2015, October 19). Homan square revealed: How Chicago police 'disappeared' 7,000 people. *The Guardian*. Retrieved from https://www.theguardian.com/us-news/2015/oct/19/homan-square-chicago-police-disappeared-thousands.

Bhuiyan, J. (2021). LAPD ended predictive policing programs amid public outcry. A new effort shares many of their flaws. *The Guardian*. Retrieved from https://www.theguardian.com/us-news/2021/nov/07/lapd-predictive-policing-surveillance-reform.

Cityoflancasterca.org. (2024). *Rex Parris, Mayor of Lancaster, LA County*. Retrieved from https://www.cityoflancasterca.org/government/city-officials/city-council/mayor-r-rex-paris.

Daily Journal. (2012). *Section 8 Tenants Unwelcome*. Retrieved from https://www.dailyjournal.com/articles/288901-section-8-tenants-unwelcome.

Havorlson, J. T. (2022). *The Impact of Police Unions on the Prosecution of Officers, Legitimacy, and Reform* [Unpublished Master's Thesis]. Southern Illinois University Carbondale. Retrieved from https://opensiuc.lib.siu.edu/cgi/viewcontent.cgi?article=2488&context=gs_rp.

Kraska, P. (2007). Militarization and policing: Its relevance to 21st century police. *Policing*, pp. 1–13. https://doi.org/10.1093/police/pam065.

Outland, R. (2019). Symbolic meaning of violence: Urban African-American adolescent males perspectives. *Journal of African American Studies*, *23*(3), 233–255. https://doi.org/10.1007/s12111-019-09440-y.

Outland, R., Noel, T., Rounsville, K., Boatwright, T., Waleed, C., & Abraham, A. (2020). Living with trauma: Impact of police killings on the lives of the family and community of child and teen victims. *Current Psychology*, *41*, 7059–7073. Retrieved from https://rdcu.be/cbkti.

Shaw, N. (2021). Aaron Brandon's death at the hands of an off-duty police officer raises questions. *New York Times Student Journalism Institute*. Retrieved from https://nyc21.nytimes-institute.com/aaron-brandon-ba8df93f3c03.

Stop LAPD Spying. (2018). Before the bullet hits the body: Dismantling predictive policing in LA. *Stop LAPD Spying Coalition*. Retrieved from https://stoplapdspying.org/wp-content/uploads/2018/05/Before-the-Bullet-Hits-the-Body-May-8–2018.pdf.

5

MAKING SENSE OF THE SENSELESS

Where Do We Go From Here

Police killings of youth can be described and understood as a pressing epidemic in U.S. society. This phenomenon should be understood as more than single occurring events or acts of mistaken consequence. With more than 1,000+ citizens being killed, or losing their lives, at the hands of police each year for the past decade (Mapping Police Violence, 2024; Outland, 2021), this catastrophe must be dealt with directly and with a poignant scientific analysis. Thus, in order to end police killings of citizens in this country, first, the purpose of policing in the United States from a historical lens (Abu-Jamal, 2016; Umoja, 2013; Vitale, 2018), along with armed-resistance to this form of State-sanctioned violence (Bukhari, 2010; Hess, 2000; Hill, 2010; Muntaqim, 2020), must be understood. The authors attempted to accomplish this goal in Chapter 2. Next, an assessment of the impact of the phenomenon on human functioning should follow (Aymer, 2016; Chaney & Robertson, 2013; Halvorson, 2022; Outland et al., 2020; Schweikert, 2020; Seigal, 2018a). In Chapter 4, readers learn about the lived experiences, meanings, and perceptions of survivors in the aftermath of youth killed by police. These firsthand stories provide vital information about "what happens" when a youth is killed by police. Finally, remedies to address this epidemic must be drawn. The authors attempt to collectivize this information in Chapter 4 as well, vis-à-vis participants' narratives. The researchers are clear that if others were to pick up and assess the dataset used, perhaps different thematic schemes and understandings would transpire.

Yet, due to the reality that limited to no qualitative inquiries have been conducted on this phenomenon, the researchers carry the belief and

DOI: 10.4324/9781003665915-5

responsibility to conduct such works, as well as present the outcomes to the general public. In the following sections, we discuss several major themes in relation to the body of works from Chapter 2. Furthermore, we include recommendations and strategies to address police killings as well as restitution and reparation for survivors of these atrocities. We conclude the section by highlighting limitations of this project, along with solutions to address them.

Impact of Youth Killed by Police on Family and Loved Ones

No parent, sibling, grandparent, aunt, uncle, cousin, and friend want to experience a child taken by a traumatic death. The mental, emotional, and at times, physical wounds are long-standing and can have dramatic effects on the individual's personhood. A mother's horror, a father's fear, and a sibling's sorrow become more heightened when the purveyors of violence are the same forces who were assigned by law to protect children: The police. While those who loved the child will remember him as a "good kid," "loving friend," or "role model for youth," the police only deemed the child as a criminal, thug, and lawbreaker who was deserving of an untimely death. The child on a bike is signaled by cops as a grown man and shot down in a Laser Zone in LA. Another child is deemed and treated as a street thug or gang member, beaten and tortured in back alleyways, and later gunned down for assuming to have flung an object at a moving unmarked patrol car. Justified homicides. Stolen dreams is what a mother has to endure, when she can no longer touch, smell, feel, and talk with her young man about his future, dreams, and aspirations. Some parents will no longer become grandparents, and girlfriends to wives of their deceased spouse. Moreover, a child will grow up and never get to meet her father, which constitutes an immediate adverse childhood experience for the developing youth. We can conclude that police killings of youth create a ripple effect that can be understood as a cycle of trauma, hardship, and destruction. For those who loved and cared for the deceased youth, the pain and suffering endured are inevitable. Many participants expressed and described the impact of losing a loved one violently at the hands of police. For example, participants discussed depression, anger, regret, despair, and even feelings of guilt. The impact of losing a loved one to police violence reverberated throughout communities where child and teen victims resided, to the geographical areas where they were killed by police, and to family and friend circles that knew and loved them unconditionally. Therefore, we refer to these numerous reverberations of pain and trauma on loved ones and communities as the *ripple effect.*

Furthermore, for family and loved ones who lose a child to police killings, we can conclude that there is no justice in the criminal justice system, but only continued encounters of humiliation and injustice. For instance, some families spoke of being denied access to view, identify, and touch their deceased child after being killed by police. Furthermore, mothers further suggested being disrespected, belittled, and humiliated by judges and officials during court hearings. In addition, the sad part is that despite a family member or loved one traumatically losing a child, it was rare to never that anyone from the courts demonstrated empathy and compassion to survivors. To experience months, and at times years, of disrespect and humiliation by the courts, only in the end for the courts to deem the police officer's actions *JUSTIFIED* (Halvorson, 2022; Schweikert, 2020), only acts as further fuel to the emotional and mental fire. In other words, further pain and suffering is distributed to families by the court ruling of the officer(s) being Justified for taking the life of a child. The act by the courts to Justify the killing of citizens by police, especially in regard to youth victims, can be understood as an act of *DeValuing Black Life*. In this regard, Black, Brown, Indigenous, and Poor White lives Do Not Matter (Abu-Jamal, 2017), simply being that these youthful lives were taken by those players who act as the security wing of the State: The police (Seigal, 2018b). For example, Micol Seigal (2018b), in her profound book, *Violence Works: State Power and the Limits of Police*, makes the following connection between legitimating police violence and State power:

> Police legitimacy fortifies and rests upon state legitimacy because the two are rough expressions of each other. Police and state are differentiated by degree: police are the human-scale expression of the state . . . State and state capacity are "phenomena of police"; "discourses of governance . . . are quintessentially discourses of the police." "As a core component of the state's monopoly on the legitimate means of coercion, police practices epitomize sovereignty in action"; or simply, regardless of some exceptional status we might like to delineate with the notion of "corruption," police are "fundamentally political".
>
> *(pp. 9–10)*

In addition, the devaluing of the lives of survivors is further denoted as a result of police cover-ups in the aftermath of the killings. Some family members suggested police hiding evidence and pertinent information about a child's death by police. At times, this included hiding or covering up physical evidence on the deceased child's body. Such cover-ups must be understood as internal workings, which can be deemed as further attempts to Justify *how* and *why* the child lost his life to police. Police cover-ups, which can be described as police corruption, can be situated as major causes to why youth in urban settings hold fear, apprehension, and distrust for the police (Outland, 2021). These forms of police corruption align with Vitale's (2018) depiction of police corruption and incompetence as naturally situated in the origins of U.S. policing. For instance, he reminds us that police, historically, were chosen based on their political connections and bribery, received no civil service exam or training, and often accepted payments from gamblers and, later, bootleggers as a major source of income. Such a system, also known as being "On The Take" (pp. 38–39) by police, remained standard practice in many major police departments until the 1970s. Thus, we can conclude that police cover-ups and corruption in the aftermath of youth killed by police are not instances of a *few bad cops* but quite the opposite: Being *on the Take* is a natural and historical practice of U.S. policing.

Finally, survivors of youth killed by police do not choose to become actively engaged to combat police terrorism, but are chosen. In other words, family members of deceased youth, oftentimes, are unaware of the frequency and gravity of police brutality in their community. However, after their youthful loved one is taken by police, in one way or another, survivors may feel obligated and responsible to join the struggle. This responsibility seems directly tied to their desire and passion to pursue justice and police accountability for their deceased child or loved one. Moreover, family members have found support, grace, and an ability to relate with other survivors of police killings, primarily mothers. These spaces not only allow survivors the opportunity to heal, discuss, and process what occurred they further receive opportunities to build alliances with other community members who are also seeking justice for their deceased loved one. This process can be described as a *Collective Alliance for Justice (CAJ)*. Because most families believed that holding police accountable means them being held to the same standard as normal citizens for taking the life of another, the CAJ, such as MOBB in Chicago for Ms. Nicole, can act as an important resource and support for survivors in the aftermath of youth killed by police. Although family members who become activists are convinced that their involvement will not bring back the life of their loved one, they further carry a belief that such activity may prevent a child from being killed by police in the future.

The formation of Collective Alliances for Justice (CAJ) following police killings remains a historical and contemporary phenomenon, usually consisting of survivors of these atrocities. For instance, The Rainbow Coalition, fueled by Chairman Fred Hampton, a BPP member, evolved due to police terrorism and poverty plaguing poor Black, Brown, and White communities in the Northeast United States. This formation included the BPP, White Patriots (predominantly poor White members), and Young Lords (López, 2019). Moreover, they organized across racial and ethnic lines, with primary aims to combat police brutality, poverty, and substandard housing

(Independent Lens, 2021). In addition, following the kidnapping and lynching of Emmett Till by two White racist vigilantes, his mother, Mamie Till-Mobley, sacrificed her life to speak her son's truth and experience in court due to ongoing threats from White racist vigilantes and sheriffs. As a result, led by T.R. Howard, Ruby Hurley, Medgar Evers, and Amzie Moore, they developed armed protection and security apparatuses to protect Ms. Till-Mobley at home and while escorted to court (Umoja, 2013). In contemporary times, parents or relatives of youth and adults killed by police, including but not limited to, Michael Brown (Madeson, 2024; Wimbley, 2024), Tamir Rice (Ellis, 2020; Perry, 2021), Daniel Prude (Aljazeera, 2020; Shackford, 2020), Breonna Taylor (Blackburn, 2022; Greg, 2024), and George Floyd (Associated Press, 2021; Sykes & Taukolo, 2024), all have found themselves advocating for justice and accountability on behalf of their family member's sudden death by police. As a result, we can conclude that collective unity and alliances against police corruption, abuse, and terrorism are continued historical and contemporary responses by survivors, as well as the masses, in the aftermath of police killings.

Impact of Youth Killed by Police on Community Members and Activists

Contextualizing Policing in the United States

Police killings of youth must first be understood as not existing in a vacuum or an isolated part of U.S. history. Yet, this phenomenon should be situated within the larger historical context of policing in the United States which the roots of this institution are directly tied to colonial practices of the Extermination of Indigenous people of Turtle Island, Land and Resource theft (Dunbar-Ortiz, 2015; Hill, 2010), as well as the enslavement of Africans (Abu-Jamal, 2016; Zinn, 2003). These connections by critical scholars provide readers a clarity surrounding the purpose, etiology, and continuity of policing in the United States (Umoja, 2013; Vitale, 2018). For example, several participants in this study understood policing in their communities as being grounded in violence, unlawfulness, and in some instances, murder of community dwellers. Without analyzing and taking note of the history of U.S. policing, then, we are left with the surface-level, monotonous, discourse of "good and bad cop." This type of ahistorical discourse fails to make connections between historical and contemporary purposes of policing, which have remained 1) to protect the assets of the ruling elite (including human chattel during the historical enslavement of Africans by European colonizers), 2) to maintain the status quo of the ruling elite as economic, political, and social controllers of the working-class populous, and finally, 3) the maintenance of social control (i.e., qualming of working-class uprising historically) through state-sanctioned violence, terror, and punishment. As some authors have argued, these lenses toward policing in the United States can assist readers in making sense of the purpose and goal of policing, at local, national, and international levels (Kraska, 2007; Seigal, 2018a; Vitale, 2018).

Structural Violence and Policing in the United States

Policing as a form of structural violence was captured as an important theme in this work. In order to make sense of this aspect of policing, a few factors must be considered. First, scholars such as Dylan Rodriguez (2021, 2023) and others have helped readers understand "why" policing can be understood as an inhumane employment occupation. If we are sincere about this understanding, we can conclude that there is not an occupation that exists when an individual can kill or take the life of another at work, and in most cases, the act is deemed *JUSTIFIED* and the killer is granted impunity by the State. According to Mapping Police Violence (2024), most police killings occur in low-income and poverty-ridden areas. This information is key to understanding the economic incentives surrounding this type of social control by policing. For example, most, if not all, government housing in poor and low-income urban centers are owned and controlled by outside forces, or individuals who do not reside in these communities. Thus, the goal of these outside forces is not to uplift the people or redevelop these communities for current residents. In practice, the goal of those who control the economy of urban centers is primarily interested in "turning a profit" via the economic exploitation of poor people. In this regard, crime in these urban centers become more than acts of survival, but can be described as the *vehicle to maintain the continuation of profits* for those who control low-income poor communities. How is this the case? When a supposed crime happens in poor communities, the State has designed a system of structured violence for poor people to 1) lose social and economic control once becoming an inmate of the State and 2) jobs, employment, along with exuberant fines for the poor, are all part of a process of making money, or turning a profit, off poor people's supposed "Crimes and Punishment" (Herivel & Wright, 2007, pp. 27–35). Thus, the current system of structural violence in the United States, which includes everyday poverty, policing, failing schools, and the prison industrial complex, is currently structured to generate mass profit for the ruling elite, or 1% of the U.S. population. Rural communities where prisons and jails are continuously built have further generated from this arrangement due to policing and correctional officers remaining some of the highest paying jobs in these communities (Herivel & Wright, 2007, pp. 90–98).

Herivel and Wright, in their seminal work titled *Prison Profiteers: Who Makes Money Off of Mass Incarceration?*, describe these urban communities as *Million-Dollar Blocks.* According to the authors, Million-Dollar Blocks can be understood as a concentrated area of blocks and neighborhoods where most people sent to state prisons come from these urban communities. They suggest that millions of state tax dollars are spent to confine poor Black and Brown residents of Brooklyn, NY, primarily residing in "East New York, Bedford-Stuyvesant, and Brownsville" (p. 30), at times ranging from $1 to $5 million in annual spending. Furthermore, the authors contend that

> prison spending maps highlight the fact that money spent on million-dollar blocks winds up in another part of the state – far from the scene of the crime. In New York state, about 60 percent of prisoners come from NYC, but virtually every prison is located upstate, in rural towns and villages, places like Attica, Dannemora, and Malone.
>
> *(Herivel & Wright, 2007, p. 31)*

They conclude with a quote by Todd Clear, a professor at John Jay College of Criminal Justice, with the following: "People who live on Park Avenue give a lot of money to people who live in Auburn, NY, in order to watch people who live in Brooklyn for a couple of years–and send them back damaged" (p. 31). Thus, we can conclude that the system of structural violence in the United States has a stake in maintaining the everyday struggles of poverty and survival in low-income and under-resourced urban centers.

This leads to our discourse on predictive policing and Operation LASER. As we have understood, predictive policing can be denoted as the utility of "advanced technology" by police and law enforcement to identify and surveil potential "crime" before it occurs, and in turn, prevent its occurrence. In this vein, the police acts as a supposed preventative force of crime in low-income urban centers predominantly populated by the Black and Brown populace. As we have seen in this study, projects such as Operation LASER "do not" prevent and/or deter possible acts of crime from occurring. Its primary goal is to propagandize the use of advanced technology by police to the community, in order to, as stated eloquently by Jamie Garcia in this work, "legitimize and justify police terror, violence, and brutality in low-income urban centers." This practice by policing is similar to the type of police reform that occurred following the killing of Black teens by police, such as Michael Brown by Ferguson police and Laquan McDonald by Chicago police. Specifically, police body cameras, use of drones and mechanical dogs, police review boards, and some officers firing and rehiring on the force were suggested as reforms to address the ongoing police terror in poor Black and Brown communities (Equal Justice Initiative (EJI), 2019; NCJA, 2024; Preston & Bordon, n.d.). Thus, with a close examination of "data-driven" police operations such as Operation LASER, these projects carry fault and ineffectiveness, often leading to the killing and/or capturing of the wrong person, and in turn, the police department are moved to find the best story, scenario, and/or experiences to *Justify* why they killed a resident, especially Black and Brown youth (Bhuiyan, 2021; Puente, 2019; Vargas, 2023).

In a capitalist society, being poor and living in government housing or low-income urban centers is a crime. A crime in the sense that despite an individual waking up daily to work a low-paying job, or one's commitment to rearing, nurturing, and guiding youth, as this study noted, simply living in poor conditions increases one's possibility of being targeted by police violence and terror. As some authors denote, the police can be understood as an occupying force or source of containment in low-income Black and Brown communities (Kraska, 2007; Mowatt, 2022). Furthermore, racial profiling, stop-and-frisk practices, as well as police brutality, harassment, and at times killings, can be understood as outcomes of continued police containment of poor urban centers. Mowatt (2022) reminds us,

> The cop is not a civilian in spite of collecting a check, clocking in and out, and shopping at the grocery store. The powers given to the cop render them within the apparatus of the State but above all other apparatuses with their dispatching of force and death.
>
> *(p. 234)*

Due to common practices by banks and money lenders that either deny loans to low-income residents or provide them with exuberant interest rates attached, it appears that a major goal of those who "own" low-income urban centers is to keep them poor, desolate of resources, and in turn, remaining a space in time for police containment and occupation. Mowatt (2022) concludes that "the connection between the violence from the police, violence from the State, and violence that is fundamentally a part of racialisation is the same violence, one violence by the State in the sole interests of capital" (pp. 234–235). Thus, since most low-income communities are owned by capitalists and the police are designed to protect the assets and property of capitalists, we can conclude that capitalists have designed a desolate zone for continued profit generation as a result of the so-called crime that exists in these communities. In turn, such desolate zones are secured by police.

FIGURE 5.1 Corner of Century Boulevard and Magnolia Square in Los Angeles, CA where a youth victim was killed by police.

Struggle for Justice, Community Organizing, and the Meaning of Activism

A community's struggle for justice following the untimely death of a youth is more than an isolated event or action. According to this study, the struggle for justice appears to be a protracted one over time, involving many community stakeholders and family, and primarily fueled by community organizers and organizing. Community organizing in this regard are organizers' efforts to bring impacted people together to decide on the best form of reparation to the damage caused to their deceased youthful loved one (Independent Lens, 2021, p. 21). Indeed, this kind of struggle for justice is reparatory in nature, or can be described as reparations: The process in which those who have been wronged and victimized must decide on the appropriate remedy for their healing. As we know, there can be no healing without justice. For example, in contemporary times, due to family and community members' challenges to find legal and political justice for their family member killed by police in the current judicial arrangement, this social and political conundrum has led families to seek justice in civil lawsuits, which in turn, primarily equates to economic restitution. In this regard, Justice can be understood in forms of civil lawsuits that are settled upon by families and the police department, which typically includes a non-disclosure agreement (NDA), hindering families and loved ones from future public discussion about the case of their family member killed by police. In addition, this study further highlighted cases in LA County, in which organizers and activists were able to reach a $2.1 billion settlement due to continued brutality, harassment, and discrimination performed by the LA County Sheriff's Department toward the local poor Black and Brown community. From the families of Michael Brown, Sandra Bland, and many others, receiving economic restitution in forms of civil lawsuit settlements by the police has become a common form of Justice over the past decade. News Outlets and recent reports have attempted to document civil lawsuit settlement payouts due to police misconduct and abuse. For example, the Washington Post (2024) collected data on nearly "40,000 payments at 25 of the nation's largest police and sheriff's departments within the past decade, documenting more than $3.2 billion spent to settle claims" (Alexander et al., 2022, para. 6). Furthermore, the Times (2024) recently reported that the New York Police Department (NYPD), alone, paid out more than $500 million in civil settlements over the last six years, including nearly $115 million in 2023 (Meko, 2024, para. 2). NYPD, known as one of the most overfunded police forces on the planet, having received billions of dollars from mayors and elected officials, all the while maintaining an extensive record of torture, killings, and brutality of local residents (James, 2023). In making sense of this form of Justice, two points are worth highlighting: First, working-class taxpayer dollars are used to pay the civil lawsuit settlements levied by citizens against police (Alexander et al., 2022). We must remain mindful that this outcome is a result of a LEOBOR provision that imposes the payment of said fines on citizens, according to the following: "City governments paying legal fees of officers involved in instances of alleged misconduct" (Halvorson, 2022, p. 12). Second, since police are found *JUSTIFIED* for any wrongful behavior (Halvorson, 2022), and in turn, permitted by the courts to return to work, the idea of Justice in this form, primarily due to the loss of youthful life involved, is highly questionable and worth further investigation (Schweikert, 2020).

We conclude this discussion surrounding the *Meaning of Activism*. As we suggest in other sections, the primary aim of activism is to identify, analyze, and in turn, move toward abolishing all forms of structural violence in society, including police terrorism. We are reminded of Angela Davis's (2003) work, *Are Prisons Obsolete?* (*Which remains a pressing question in contemporary times*), when she reminds us of the historical period when most people could not imagine, nevertheless experience, a society without African Chattel Slavery (Davis, 2003). In simple terms, this was primarily due to common peoples', especially White ones, overreliance, dependency, and control of human chattel as an institution, along with the exponential production of economic profits for slavers (Rodney, 1982). Some critics and open-thinkers may argue that the same social, political, and economic scenarios are primary reasons for most people's difficulty to envision a public safety apparatus different from the police. Specifically, as we know, most societies and communities rely on policing to address all problems, whether they be social, emotional, psychological, interpersonal, and/or violent encounters. The problem with police intervention in most encounters is that they are only trained to deal with, address, and utilize "Violence." Mariam Kaba (2021), in her seminal work, *We Do This Till We Free Us*, reminds us,

> There is not a single era in U.S. history in which the police were not a force of violence against Black people. Policing in the South emerged from the slave patrols in the 1700s and 1800s that caught and returned runaway slaves. In the North, the first municipal police departments in the mid 1800s helped quash labor strikes and riots against the rich. Everywhere, police have suppressed marginalized populations to protect the status quo.
>
> *(p. 14)*

Furthermore, a prime example of this visual and observational evidence can be captured in the documentary film, *Do Not Resist* (Atkinson, 2016). This film is a primer of how police are ***conditioned*** into, educated, and rewarded for their utility of Violence against poor Black, Brown, and White communities. When considering these contemporary aspects of policing, the meaning of organizing is no longer limited to the visual, singing, and holding hands in the aftermath of a youth killed by police. Plain and Simple, Organizing must revolve around ending "police containment, oppression, and violence" of suffering people: ***Structural and Deputized Violence.*** In doing so, perhaps organizers are the vanguard, leaders, and movers of reparation and justice for survivors of youth killed by police, while collectivizing the masses to analyze, embrace, and in turn, implement solutions that lead to restorative justice and abolition of police oppression and violence.

In the following section, we extend recommendations that may lead to the transformation of policing in the United States. Prior to reviewing them, please be clear that these recommendations are only from our perspective, and perhaps, there are many other remedies to consider to end police killings of youth in the United States. However, these recommendations can become modes of study, analysis, and application for the concerned

Organizer. History and those who were part of it have extended important lessons and information to address the oppression of society. Police killings of youth and adults with impunity, as a form of structural and deputized violence in the United States, must be addressed.

Transforming Policing in the United States: Recommendations

Prior to presenting and discussing information in the following sections, it must be stated that Defunding Police, as well as Abolishing Policing, are not logical conclusions for simple reasons. First, Defunding police is highly improbable due to the historical and contemporary nature of policing, which they operate as an extension of state-sanctioned power. Thus, the State, along with ruling class elites, will not "defund" their security apparatus, but do the opposite: Give them more funding! This was demonstrated with concision following the election of U.S. President Joe Biden. Before his campaign, he supported organizers' call to defund the police. After he won, he gave the entire police union large sums of state funding (Gangitano, 2023; Ludwig, 2022). In addition, Abolishing policing, or the form of public safety in most communities in this country, again, remains impractical, without alternatives. Growing up and living in a police-state, most poor Black and Brown people only know how to dial "911" during the case of an emergency, which is the direct line to the police. Thus, if there does not exist an alternative form of public safety in low-income Black and Brown communities, then most people will continue to rely on police to intervene in all communal affairs, which we should expect Violence as a primary remedy.

Thus, here we discuss several points that can lead to the transformation of policing, and in turn, put an end to police killings of youth and adults in the United States. First, an Independent Investigation of policing in the United States, separate those conducted by Federal, State, and Local officials, must occur. In turn, this inquiry can foster the construction of a Summative Report that provides a process for the *Dismantling of Police Unions.* Specifically, Organizers, along with families and communities impacted by police killings of their loved ones, can become strategic allies in order to analyze and investigate *policing as a culture* as well as the *police union*. The police union can be understood as the political body of the police culture, which they operate to develop and implement laws, policies, and mandates that protect and *Justify* police wrongdoing, misconduct, and killings (Dharmapala et al., 2018; Halvorson, 2022). Thus, the necessary evidence, materials, stories, and information must be gathered and compiled to educate and organize concerned populace regarding the necessity and urgency to dismantle the police union. The dismantling of the police union, in turn, could have an immediate impact on the economic security of the police culture (which we are reminded is paid by taxpayers; Alexander et al., 2022) as well as policies and laws such as LEOBORs (Halvorson, 2022, which we present and describe in Chapter 2) that protect unlawful policing and corruption. Furthermore, this transformation may permit local community members with more political power to determine which forces can and cannot act as security personnel in their neighborhoods, thus transferring some of the political power on the ground from the police back to the people.

Necessity for Local and Community Control of Public Safety by Residents (i.e., Mental, Social, Physical Safety and Wellness)

Public safety, or the experience and feeling of safety in one's home, vehicle, and community, must become human rights for all communities in the United States. A human right in the sense that all people who reside in the United States must carry the right to protect themselves, their family, and fellow neighbors. Such protection by the public must extend to disrupt and prevent unlawful police terrorism, brutality, and killings in poor Black, Brown, Indigenous, and marginalized communities. Furthermore, alternative solutions and interventions to address the emotional, mental, and domestic challenges that exist among residents in urban and rural areas must become normalized. For instance, following the nationally known killings of Black people in the United States, including George Floyd and Daniel Prude, local communities developed policies and programs that permit mental health and social workers to intervene during an individual's mental, emotional, and domestic crisis. These service providers are more likely to intervene in these situations 1) without the use of lethal force and 2) with compassion and empathy toward the individual(s) involved (Alliance for Rights and Recovery, 2023; Evans, 2021). Thus, if a perpetrator and victim are involved, they are more likely to *Live* following an intervention by trusted service providers when compared to police. In this regard, for most residents, there becomes a clear separation between the need for service providers' support and public safety intervention. As Frantz Fanon (2004) noted, the psychiatric clinics will continue to be filled due to the existence of a colonial situation, or the colonizer maintaining social, economic, and political control of the colonized. Thus, we must note that as long as poverty, crime, prisons as big-business, warfare monopoly, along with capitalist unchecked profits on the suffering of the oppressed remain static, then we can conclude that this colonial arrangement will continue to produce mental, emotional, social, and physical challenges among the colonized populace. More policing and containment is not the solution to this arrangement, but a federal government intervention to 1) redistribute wealth from the 1% affluent class to poor people, 2) transform the living, wellness, and economic conditions of poor and marginalized communities, and 3) provide equitable access to resources and living standards similar to those that exist in predominantly White suburban middle-class communities. For instance, Mowatt (2022) as well as Herivel and Wright (2007) remind readers of how according to geographical mapping, concentrated urban locales where majority of poor Black and Brown people reside are hotbeds for police containment and occupation, unlawful raids, exuberant arrests and nonviolent convictions, as well as million-dollar investments to maintain the cycle of incarceration and recidivism in these areas. As a result, in similar fashion as the State tends to target these communities for Crime and Punishment, the same resources, economic structures, and ideas for development can be utilized to target these communities for *Economic and Political Transformation*. Critics will continue to remind readers that the State always seems to find resources and funding to contain, capture, and mass incarcerate poor Black, Brown, and Indigenous people in the United States and abroad. The same urgency must be taken by these political actors to extend the necessary mandates for the complete reparation, upliftment, as well as economic and political stability of poor people in the United States and beyond.

If citizens are convinced that the police, as a government organization, must remain in the community, then perhaps it is necessary for police officers to be mandated to reside in the communities where they police. For instance, policy can be developed to require police officers to reside in a 5 to 10 mile radius from communities where they police. This residential mandate would mean that officers are no longer permitted to travel 25 to 50 miles across town to "protect and serve" residents in which they have no contact. This residential mandate would be quite the opposite: *police officers would protect and serve their own families, neighbors, children, friends, and their playmates from the community.* By policing people who reside in close proximity, it is possible that police may carry a different posture and approach when intervening in the so-called crime by residents. For instance, if a neighbor or officer's child's best friend is reported to have stolen a vehicle in the community, the intervening officer may be more inclined to intervene "without" the use of lethal force or acting as judge and jury in a given situation. Thus, the police officer may be more inclined to use self-constraint and humane practices when policing someone of familiarity. This residential mandate of police may also reduce the number of police killings in the United States, in this arrangement, the police would be killing residents of their own community instead of those in which they have limited to no contact. Furthermore, if police officers hold residence in or around low-income areas, then they may develop a deeper understanding of the line of demarcation between poverty, survival, and crime in these communities, which in many cases, remains a blurred and warped perception among most police officers. Thus, they have a chance to understand the difference between crime and survival of Black, Brown, Indigenous, and poor and marginalized communities, which in turn, may increase police compassion and empathy for local residents. Moreover, residential mandates by police provide an additional layer of *social* accountability and responsibility to their local community. Specifically, police who kill someone from their community, in turn, would have to answer and provide rationales and justifications for their actions to neighbors and friends, which in these instances, would also include survivors of victims killed by police. A final note is that residential mandate of police may increase the economic stratification of urban and rural locales, being that police typically earn close to six-figure salaries and sometimes above this pay grade. Thus, the hope is for police officers to dwell in, support, and be part of the community in a similar fashion as any working-class resident.

Local Community Control of Public Safety

In concluding this section on recommendations, specifically *Transforming the Police*, we recommend a complete deconstruction and reconstruction of the structure of policing, particularly in local communities. Currently, most police departments' chain of command policies are hierarchical beginning with the mayor or city council members, the superintendent or chief of police, to other police administrators known as *brass* or *White shirts* (i.e., captains, lieutenants, sergeants, and commanders) to detectives and foot patrol or rank and file officers. The chain of command directs the *brass officers* as well as rank and file officers to follow orders given by political figures and police administrators regarding how and where to patrol (or occupy jurisdictions), respond to calls, *lawbreakers*, and public unrest/disturbances and protesters. It is important to note that rank and file do not decide *officially* how to respond to these tasks, instead they are given *orders* to follow by their superiors. Furthermore, in most communities and jurisdictions, everyday citizens and community members typically do not participate, nor are they included, in the decision-making process; thus, we argue that this chain of command must be inclusive of the citizens of these communities with decision-making and review authority of public safety. More specifically, we recommend that local community public safety should be organized, led, and represented by the people who reside in these communities. To that end, we recognize that this transition from government-controlled public safety to community-led public safety cannot occur overnight; therefore, we recommend a timely transition *with all deliberate speed* of power to the community and the people.

Elimination/Abolition of Policies and Police Unions That Support Qualified Immunity and Lack of Accountability Following Police-Involved Killings of a Person

Policies that uphold Qualified Immunity, or Lack of accountability and wrongdoing following a police-involved homicide, must be abolished and discontinued. These policies include those that provide police departments with political and governing power to investigate, assess, and make a decision about the lawful or unlawful behaviors of their fellow officer. These policies can be understood as the remnants of the *Police Unions of the Fraternity of Police (FOP)* along with the *Law Enforcement Bill of Rights (LEOBORs)*. We must be clear that these policies and structures are primers that protect and privilege police in the aftermath of police misconduct and homicide. According to Halvorson's (2022) seminal work titled *The Impact of Police Unions on the Prosecution of Officers, Legitimacy, and Reform,* LEOBORs constitute six provisions that remain problematic, which include the following:

> Early disqualification of misconduct complaints, delaying interrogations of officers accused of misconduct, giving officers access to additional information before an interrogation (in comparison to criminal suspects who are not sworn officers), limiting disciplinary consequences for officers accused of misconduct, city governments paying legal fees of officers involved in instances of alleged misconduct, and preventing the retainment of an officer's disciplinary history.

The author further suggests that a major reason police homicides rarely result in prosecution and conviction could be due to police unions (p. 1) along with state and local clauses/policies that reflect the LEOBORs (pp. 12–13). He further reported a study by Walker (2001), which found 71% of police officers to be represented by a union. Finally, a study analyzing 81 police union contracts and 14 states that had LEOBORs, McKesson et al. (2016) found that "72 of the 81 union contracts and all of the LEOBORs had at least one of the six listed 'problematic provisions' that actively worked against improving police accountability" (Halvorson, 2022, p. 12). We can conclude that a combination of Qualified Immunity, police unions, and LEOBORs makes it more difficult, or impossible, for the courts and civilians to prove an officer's guilt and levy consequences in the aftermath of a youth killed by police. Thus, of the average 1,000+ victims of police homicide in the United States each year over the past decade, holding the highest body count in 2023 of 1300+ citizen deaths by police (Mapping Police Violence, 2024; Washington Post, 2024), qualified immunity policies and structures continue to *JUSTIFY* and protect police actions (i.e., the officer killed a child due to fear for his life – Schweikert, 2020). For instance, Schweikert's (2020) scholarship titled *Qualified Immunity: A Legal, Practical, and Moral Failure* suggests the following:

> Qualified immunity has been disastrous as a matter of policy. Victims of egregious misconduct are often left without any legal remedy simply because there does not happen to be a prior case on the books involving the exact same sort of misconduct. By undermining public accountability at a structural level, the doctrine also hurts the law enforcement community by denying police the degree of public trust and confidence they need to do their jobs safely and effectively.
>
> *(p. 1)*

Thus, such policies and structures must be eliminated and abolished. As noted in this research, if the police take the life of a resident, then she should be held to the same standards and practices as any common resident who commits a similar offense. Participants understood that in reality, police are not above the law. Yet, according to the LEOBORs' six provisions, standards of policy, police unions, as well as a biased judicial system, position police as the security arm of the State that operates with impunity (Halvorson, 2022). Thus, the elimination of LEOBORs at the local, state, and national levels along with dismantling of police unions, may result in police being immediately arrested, booked, as well as granted bond (if warranted) and a jury trial by their peers, in the aftermath of a police-involved homicide.

Furthermore, the officer "should not" be paid while the case is pending, which this outcome, in many cases, is due to clauses of the LEOBORs. Specifically, one provision of the LEOBORs suggests the following: "city governments paying legal fees of officers involved in instances of alleged misconduct" (Halvorson, 2022, p. 12). Here, local and state police departments operating under this provision are permitted to manipulate the language of local policy to ensure that taxpayer dollars levy the legal costs, fees, and payouts to survivors of the deceased, as well as officers, accrued following police-involved killings. In addition, the officer should be tried by a *Jury of Peers* from the communities 1) where she patrols, 2) where she resides, and 3) where the police-involved homicide occurred. This blend of jury members can provide an equitable assessment of the police-involved homicide and potential consequences. Finally, the case can proceed as any homicide or murder trial, and if found guilty by a jury of his peers, the officer should be given a similar sentence for murder by the courts, as would most common residents (i.e., 25 years to life, etc.). At this time, the following LEOBORs' provision protects police from receiving such consequences: "limiting disciplinary consequences for officers accused of misconduct" (Halvorson, 2022, p. 12). As a result, the elimination of LEOBORs, along with police unions as a structural shield of protection, may lead to the pursuit of justice by families within the judicial structure that determines most ***homicide trials by residents of the community***. Such judicial transformation can lead to just and equitable outcomes for the 1,000s of survivors of police killings in the United States each year, including survivors of youth killed by police.

The Development of Armed and Trained Local Militia Designed to Protect and Defend the Community Against Police and Vigilante Racist Terrorism

Concerned community members can form local armed and trained militias and groups to observe and disrupt unlawful practices of police in their communities. These militias can be diverse in race, class, gender, and sexual identity, primarily considering the identity stratification of members within urban and rural communities. If agreed upon by a collective vote among local residents (i.e., ***Police Accountability Board (PAB) could act as an important forum to facilitate this vote***), these militias can act as alternatives to policing within local urban and rural neighborhoods. Moreover, these armed and trained community members can further act as local public safety to monitor police activities in their communities, as previously noted. For example, the Black Panther Party (BPP) for Self-Defense (Abu-Jamal, 2016), along with the Young Lords (Enck-Wanzer, 2010), historically implemented a *Police Watch Program*, or designated members to observe and disrupt unlawful police practices and abuses while patrolling low-income Black and Brown neighborhoods. More specifically, when Denzil Dowell was gunned down by a White deputy officer in Richmond, VA, the BPP "sent twenty Panthers out there armed with guns, disciplined, standing thirty or forty feet apart on every corner of the intersection" (Abu-Jamal, 2016, p. 43). They further acted as the investigative body in the aftermath of police killings of BPP members, including Lil Bobby Hutton, Mark Clark, and Chairman Fred Hampton. In addition, the American Indian Movement (AIM), as well as the Southern Freedom Struggles of the 1960s and 1970s, further used local militias to protect citizens from police harassment, brutality, and killings, including struggles against police at Wounded Knee and the Occupation of Alcatraz (Juarez, 2017; Wittstock & Salinas, n.d.). Moreover, militias and security apparatuses forged to protect the Mother of Emmett Till during court proceedings led by Medgar Evers and others (Umoja, 2013) as well as those arranged at Pine Ridge Reservation by AIM (Dog & Erdoes, 1991; Schuttler, 1991), are concrete examples of armed-resistance against state-sanctioned violence. Thus, in contemporary times, such militias must become alternatives to policing, in which proper training, political education, and use of weaponry must be part of the daily practices of a local and communal militia. Such a security force carries the potential to limit the political and authoritative powers of the police in poor urban and rural settings. In this vein, local community members can gain control to determine their experiences, interactions, and engagement with those who police, further increasing their power to define and determine public safety in their local communities.

A final note on the utility of local armed and trained militia to combat and transform police terrorism in the United States. When considering historical armed militias that took an offensive positioning toward police terrorism, such as the Black Liberation Army (BLA – Bukhari, 2010; Muntaqim, 2020) and Revolutionary Action Movement (RAM – Shoatz, 2013), one must consider whether or not these formations and their actions had any bearing on the frequency of police killings of Black and Brown people in the United States. For example, Muntaqim (2020), in his seminal work *We Are Our Own Liberators*, reminds us of casualties of life experienced by both police officers and BLA members during the U.S. government's *Counter Intelligence Program (COINTELPRO)* war against Black, Brown, Indigenous, and White organizers and freedom fighters during the 1960s and 1970s. Moreover, Russel Maroon Shoatz's (2013) profound piece titled *Maroon the Implacable* further alludes to the reality of armed-resistance militias acting as beacons and models for the local community, according to the following:

> We (*Black Unity Council (BUC) of Philadelphia, PA*) especially liked their (RAM) emphasis on armed self-defense! At that time, RAM was very active in Philly. Their cultural workers, and semi clandestine paramilitary arm called the *Black Guard (BG)*, had a center close to our neighborhood, and we would always hang there. They had regular seminars, history/cultural classes, karate classes . . . In addition, they had a liberation school that the BUC planned to emulate.
>
> *(p. 68)*

As a result of experiencing "casualties on both sides," it is worth future inquiry and investigation to determine whether police involvement in domestic wars against activists and organizers can reduce the number of everyday residents that are killed by police in the United States. Thus, as noted in the historical lessons of the Civil Rights Freedom Struggle, BPP, Young Lords, and the BLA, the goal of such formations was to provide security, protection, and safety for local residents. Such public safety, primarily considering our contemporary moment when an estimated 1,000+ people are killed by police each year, must include protection from police terrorism, harassment, brutality, and unlawful behaviors, which can become normalized and consistent practices for local armed and trained militias.

The Necessity for Restitution and Reparation Justice for Survivors of Police Killings

In concluding this section on recommendations, it is worthy to consider the necessity for *Restitution and Reparation Justice* for survivors of police killings in the U.S. Restitution and Reparation Justice can be understood as an intervention or program designed to support and work with survivors of police killings according to the impact of this phenomenon on their daily lives. For instance, a body of literature over time denotes the impact of police-involved homicides on the mental, emotional, and physical well-being of survivors (Aymer, 2016; Chaney & Robertson, 2013; Obasogie & Newman, 2017; Outland et al., 2020; Staggers-Hakim, 2016). Moreover, police killings of citizens can further disrupt the daily lives of survivors regarding employment, housing, and finances. For example, in the current study, participants such as Precious and Mr. Mitchell discussed the disruption of a youth killed by police on their jobs and housing stability. These disruptions were a result of having to attend several court hearings that disrupted their work attendance, and more importantly, others' impositions of social labels and stigma on survivors and organizers involved with finding justice for their deceased loved ones. *In other words, simply losing a loved one to police violence can bring on a host of personal, occupational, economic, and housing challenges that survivors must navigate.* Thus, *Restitution and Reparation Justice* must be designed to meet the everyday needs of survivors in the aftermath of losing their youthful loved one. Moreover, as noted in prior sections, this form of justice involves accountability by police involved in the homicide of a youth. As we may understand, it is a major challenge for any person to begin a process of healing "without" receiving a form of justice for their loved one's sudden and tragic death.

Moving forward, a structure that can be used to facilitate *Restitution and Reparation Justice* for survivors can be produced and facilitated by trusted organizers, activists, and elders from the community. This structure should be a safe space, and ample time is allotted to "sit with" surviving families to determine their needs and desires in the aftermath of their loved one killed by police. This structure further reflects notions of *Traditional African Culture* in dealing with crime, justice, and public safety, as suggested by

Dr. Walter Rodney (1996) in his seminal work, "The *Groundings With My Brothers*." He suggests the following:

> The basic principle of justice was restitution–the object of the legal judgment being to help the wronged party rather than inflict punishment on the offender. It is significant that one hears of nothing resembling a jail within indigenous African society, nor is there any evidence of stocks, fetters, and the like . . . Capital punishment, for example, was rare, being completely absent from some societies.
>
> *(pp. 54–55)*

He further suggested that *Elders of African Traditional Culture* played self-fulfilling and socially satisfying roles in the community, which were reflective of their advanced age as bringing honor, increased respect, and authority. As a result, they were intentionally exposed to life experiences in the society, learned from specialized institutions (i.e., the Bush School), and were given secret knowledge and responsibilities to pass on teachings to the younger generation. In this vein, trusted elders of the community can play a vital role in facilitating appropriate restitution and reparation for survivors, along with consequences for the officer(s) following a police-involved homicide (Rodney, 1996, p. 55).

Thus, during a *Restitution and Reparation Justice* hearing, a panel of jurors, or trusted elders from the community, can act as the determining body of solutions or outcomes following the hearing. Organizers, freedom fighters, and activists can also contribute ideas, analyses, and solutions during this hearing. A final determinant by trusted elders on the panel of jurors can ensure that solutions and remedies of surviving families, along with a time frame to implement them, are upheld at the conclusion of the hearing. An example of solutions and strategies can include survivors receiving $5 million in restitution pay, gainful employment for ten years, and quality housing of choice. Moreover, the officer involved should be arrested, booked, and partake in a jury trial of his peers according to the equitable jury arrangement previously noted. He should also receive mandated individual mental health and trauma counseling for a minimum of one-year period, based on the discretion of the community and mental health provider. As a result, local government must be held responsible by residents to implement forms of justice and demands of survivors. Moreover, local armed militias may have a role to play in this process to ensure that the demands of survivors are met by all stakeholders involved, including police departments. After a period of time in which all remedies have been carried out successfully, a follow-up hearing with survivors and a panel of jurors can occur to determine if *survivors* are satisfied and content with local remedies, despite knowledge and fact that these remedies will not return the Life of their loved one. If survivors are content, then we can conclude that an appropriate *Restitution and Reparation Justice* process has transpired.

In conclusion, healing for survivors is a difficult reality without Justice, Restitution, and Reparation of damage and pain caused to survivors following the untimely murder of their loved one, and in turn, culprits not being held liable for the life of a deceased youth. The abovementioned recommendations can be considered as possibilities to 1) imagine, 2) transform, and 3) redesign public safety and security in low-income urban and rural communities.

Limitations and Implications for Future Research

There are several limitations to this research that are worthy of consideration. First, *Funding* was a major limitation in this study. Specifically, alongside an internal University grant that covered research assistant stipends, the majority of funds spent for the project came from the personal money of researchers. Such payments accrued included flight, room, and boarding, along with cost of living in different cities for each researcher, which varied from West to East Coast (i.e., Los Angeles versus Chicago). Thus, the project's financial obligation carries the potential to place economic strain on those involved. In order to address this limitation, future researchers should consider applying for local, state, and/or national grants that can cover project expenses. The team can apply for such grants at least one year prior to conducting the study. This will provide the team ample time to determine 1) whether the grant was received, and as a result, 2) if grant funds will be available to cover the project or if researchers will have to use personal money to cover accrued expenses during the trip(s).

Another limitation worth noting is *Time*. Specifically, during our visit to Los Angeles, CA and Chicago, IL, the team visited each city between five and seven days, which in total was a two-week trip. This factor is a limitation for several reasons. One, some participants canceled their in-person interview and wanted to reschedule the talk at a later date due to personal obligations. In addition, the team met individuals during the visit to each city who wanted to partake in the in-person talk a week or later after we departed. Since the team visited each city for one week, we were unable to reschedule some interviews, and in turn, missed important narratives of individuals impacted by youth killed by police. In this regard, the length of time for visits during the trip was a major limitation during this work. Thus, future researchers should consider extending their stay when visiting a family or community impacted by police-involved homicide of youth. Perhaps a period of three or four weeks is most practical. This time frame can provide potential interviewees opportunities to cancel and reschedule their talk at a later date. Furthermore, potential participants who sign up during the team's visit to a city can further receive an opportunity to partake in the project. This time frame can be determined and mapped out during the pre-planning phase of the project. A final solution can include conducting interviews online or via Zoom and Teams platforms. This approach can increase interviewee convenience to participate as well as comfort due to their ability to determine a self-selected or natural location for the video chat.

A final limitation relevant to this work is the *Absence of Youth Voices.* In other words, this study did not capture the narratives of children and teens impacted by their peers killed by police. This factor is a limitation being that youth, primarily between ages of 16 and 19 years, were primary targets of police killings in our original list of youth victims from 2016 and 2017. In addition, the impact of sudden and traumatic death, including police killings, on youth mental, emotional, and social wellness has been well documented (Aymer, 2016; Chaney & Robertson, 2013; Obasogie & Newman, 2017; Outland et al., 2020; Staggers-Hakim, 2016). Thus, not capturing the voices of youth impacted by their peers killed by police remains a major gap in this research and past ones. Thus, future researchers can develop youth and parent-informed consent forms, along with developmentally appropriate interview protocols, to conduct interviews with children and teens, primarily those from low-income urban and rural communities. Black, Brown, Indigenous, and White youth from these communities are directly impacted by this phenomenon (Mapping Police Violence, 2024). Thus, capturing the stories, perspectives, and lived experiences of youth on police terrorism can provide important evidence surrounding etiology, cause, and remedies to police killings in the United States. They may further have important evidence related to helping them heal and find justice in the aftermath of their beloved peer who was murdered by police (Outland et al., 2020). In other words, our youth remain an untapped resource when considering solutions to abolish police violence and reimagine public safety for under-resourced and undervalued urban and rural communities.

Conclusion

In conclusion, police killings of people remain a public health epidemic in the United States. According to Mapping Police Violence (2024), police in the United States take the lives of 1,000+ individuals each year, with 2023 being one of the highest death counts on record, with more than 1,300 victims. We must not forget that children and teen victims are part of these numbers. Thus, youth in the United States too are killed by police at alarming rates, especially those who reside in low-income, poverty-ridden, and under-resourced neighborhoods. Of all the casualties at the hands of the police, it is further relevant to note that these casualties usually occur with Impunity, or *JUSTIFIED* homicides, in which a court of pro-police personnel determines that police were in "fear of their lives" and warranted the "use of lethal or deadly force" (Miller, 2015). In each case, such a determinant by court officials continues to grant police authorization as judge and jury during routine intervention of the so-called crime. The social danger in such systemic practices of unlawfulness and support of police killings is potential to maintain and increase police terrorism of not only poor Black, Brown, and Indigenous communities but terror to the entire U.S. population, primarily our Black and Brown children and teens (Dharmapala et al., 2018; Seigal, 2018a). In order to end this domestic, historical, and contemporary terror by those who impose or uphold law on the population, a thorough and in-depth investigation of the purpose of policing must continue.

This study and book provide a historical analysis of policing in the United States, their unlawful and fear-provoking practices toward the oppressed, as well as revolutionary formations that took a stand against these activities. The book further provides contemporary knowledge on the impact of youth killed by police on family and loved ones of victims. Going forward, all concerned people, domestically and abroad, must continue to make connections between the police state, war and military apparatus abroad (primarily the locals of over 800 military bases across the globe (Costs of War, 2024)), and the ever expanding prison industrial complex in the United States (Alexander, 2012) that operates as forms of counterinsurgency and state-sanctioned hypersexualized violence against poor, radical, and revolutionary individuals (Burton, 2023). In this connection, the police can be understood as a security branch or wing of the larger apparatus, which in turn, their political power to murder people with impunity and justification is similar to the justifications used to maintain the U.S. international war machine (Abu-Jamal & Vittoria, 2018), migrant and refugee security and violence at the U.S. border (Chacon & Davis, 2006), domestic jail-prison industrial complex as a form of warfare (Burton, 2023), and the exponential economic wealth produced and gained by capitalist-ruling elite at the behest of the masses' suffering and labor exploitation (Hess, 2000; Black & Mowatt, 2024). If we intend to ever transform and/or abolish policing as we know it, then it is necessary to connect this institution to the larger security apparatus globally (Ayers, 2024). In this vein, we see clearly that policing's purpose, practice, and ideology across the board remains: To maintain social control of all oppressed people, and in turn, protect the wealth, assets, and economies of the ruling elite. Our youth are the future and we must protect them at all costs. Such protection must extend to policing in the United States and it is up to everyday citizens, organizers, educators, survivors of police killings, etc. to identify, assess, determine, and implement appropriate solutions to end this horrific parasite and callousness that continues to run amok in society. The Struggle continues . . .

References

Abu-Jamal, M. (2016). *We Want Freedom: A Life in the Black Panther Party*. Common Notions: Brooklyn, NY.

Abu-Jamal, M. (2017). *Have Black Lives Ever Mattered?* City Lights Books: San Francisco, CA.

Abu-Jamal, M., & Vittoria, S. (2018). *Murder Incorporated: Empire, Genocide, & Manifest Destiny*. Prison Radio: San Francisco, CA.

Alexander, K. L., Rich, S., & Thacker, H. (2022). The hidden billion-dollar cost of repeated police misconduct. *The Washington Post*. Retrieved from https://www.washingtonpost.com/investigations/interactive/2022/police-misconduct-repeated-settlements/.

Alexander, M. (2012). *The New Jim Crow: Mass Incarceration in the Age of Colorblindness*. New Press: New York, NY.

Aljazeera. (2020). US: Rochester mayor fires police chief over Daniel Prude's death. *Aljazeera News*. Retrieved from https://www.aljazeera.com/news/2020/9/15/us-rochester-mayor-fires-police-chief-over-daniel-prudes-death.

Alliance for Rights and Recovery. (2023). In memory of Daniel Prude, New York needs non-policemental health emergency first responders! *The Alliance for Rights and Recovery*. Retrieved from https://rightsandrecovery.org/e-news-bulletins/2023/09/20/in-memory-of-daniel-prude-new-york-needs-non-police-mental-health-emergency-first-responders/.

Associated Press. (2021). George Floyd's family holds rally, march in brother's memory. *The Associated Press, Special Series, George Floyd's Murder, One Year Later*. Retrieved from https://www.npr.org/2021/05/23/999657950/george-floyds-family-holds-rally-march-in-brothers-memory.

Atkinson, C. (2016). Do not resist. *Documentary*. Retrieved from https://www.pbs.org/pov/films/donotresist/.

Ayers, B. (2024). *When Freedom is the Question, Abolition is the Answer: Reflections on Collective Liberation*. Beacon Press: Boston, MA.

Aymer, S. R. (2016). I can't breathe: A case study – helping blackmen cope with race-related trauma stemming from police killing and brutality. *Journal of Human Behavior in the Social Environment*, *26*(3–4), 367–376. https://doi.org/10.1080/10911359.2015.1132828

Bhuiyan, J. (2021). LAPD ended predictive policing programs amid public outcry. A new effort shares many of their flaws. *The Guardian*. Retrieved from https://www.theguardian.com/us-news/2021/nov/07/lapd-predictive-policing-surveillance-reform.

Black, T., & Mowatt, R. (2024). *Laundering Black Rage: The Washing of Black Death, People, Property, and Profits*. Routledge: New York, NY.

Blackburn, P. H. (2022). Breonna Taylor's family, supporters sustain push for justice. *AP News*. Retrieved from https://apnews.com/article/ahmaud-arbery-breonna-taylor-kentucky-louisville-police-bc50866b2744793f98e026108b26d77c.

Bukhari, S. (2010). *The War Before: The True Life Story of Becoming a Black Panther, Keeping the Faith in Prison & Fighting for Those Left Behind*. The Feminist Press: New York, NY.

Burton, O. (2023). *Tip of the Spear: Black Radicalism, Prison Repression, and the Long Attica Revolt*. University of California Press: Oakland, CA.
Chacon, J. A., & Davis, M. (2006). *No One Is Illegal. Fighting Racism and State Violence on the U.S.-Mexico Border*. Haymarket Books: Chicago, IL.
Chaney, C., & Robertson, R. V. (2013). Racism and police brutality in America. *Journal of African American Studies, 17*, 480–505. https://doi.org/10.1007/s12111-013-9246-5.
Costs of War. (2024). *Costs of War Project*. Watson Institute, International & Public Affairs, Brown University. Retrieved from https://watson.brown.edu/costsofwar/figures.
Davis, A. (2003). *Are Prisons Obsolete?* Seven Stories Press: New York, NY.
Dharmapala, D., McAdams, R. H., & Rappaport, J. (2018). Collective bargaining rights and police misconduct: Evidence from Florida. *University of Chicago Public Law & Legal Theory Paper Series No. 655*. Retrieved from https://chicagounbound.uchicago.edu/public_law_and_legal_theory.
Dog, M. C., & Erdoes, R. (1991). *Lakota Woman*. Harper Perennial: New York, NY.
Dunbar-Ortiz, R. (2015). *An Indigenous Peoples' History of the United States*. Beacon Press Books: Boston, MA.
Ellis, N. T. (2020). 'You don't get over nothing like this': Mother of Tamir Rice says moving on has been painful. *USA Today*. Retrieved from https://www.usatoday.com/in-depth/news/2020/06/22/tamir-rices-mother-fights-racism-america-and-police-brutality/3116710001/.
Enck-Wanzer, D. (2010). *The Young Lords: A Reader*. New York University Press: New York, NY.
EqualJustice Initiative (EJI). (2019). Five years after Ferguson, policing reform is abandoned. *EJI*. Retrieved from https://eji.org/news/five-years-after-ferguson-policing-reform-abandoned/.
Evans, N. E. C. (2021). One year after Daniel Prude's death, has mental health care for people of color changed? *WXXI News, NPR*. Retrieved from https://www.wxxinews.org/health/2021-03-31/one-year-after-daniel-prudes-death-has-mental-health-care-for-people-of-color-changed.
Fanon, F. (2004). Colonial war and mental disorders. In Fanon, F. (Ed.), *The Wretched of the Earth*. Grove Press: New York, NY.
Gangitano, A. (2023). Biden administration announces $334M to hire police officers, improve security at schools. *The Hill*. Retrieved from https://thehill.com/homenews/administration/4289536-biden-administration-334m-police-officers-school-security/.
Greg, J. (2024). Family, activists honor the life of Breonna Taylor four years after police killing. *Spectrum News 1*. Retrieved from https://spectrumnews1.com/ky/louisville/news/2024/03/14/family--activists-honor-memory-of-breonna-taylor-four-years-later.
Halvorson, J. T. (2022). *The Impact of Police Unions on the Prosecution of Officers, Legitimacy, and Reform*. Southern Illinois University Carbondale, OpenSIUC: Carbondale. Retrieved from https://opensiuc.lib.siu.edu/gs_rp.
Herivel, T., & Wright, P. (2007). *Prison Profiteers: Who Makes Money from Mass Incarceration*. The New Press: New York, NY.
Hess, P. (2000). *Overturning the Culture of Violence*. Burning Spear Publication: St. Petersburg, FL.
Hill, G. (2010). *500 Years of Indigenous Resistance*. PM Press: Oakland, CA.
Independent Lens. (2021). The first Rainbow Coalition: Discussion guide. *Corporation for Public Broadcasting (CPB)*. Retrieved from https://

independentlens.s3.amazonaws.com/2100/The_First_Rainbow_Coalition/The-First-Rainbow-Coalition-Discussion-Guide.pdf.

James, J. (2023). *New Bones Abolition: Captive Maternal Agency and the Afterlife of Erica Garner*. Common Notions: Brooklyn, NY.

Juarez, V. (2017). AIM & the occupation of Alcatraz Island. *Historical Perspectives: Santa Clara University Undergraduate Journal of History, Series II, 22*, 7. Retrieved from https://scholarcommons.scu.edu/historical-perspectives/vol22/iss1/7.

Kaba, M. (2021). Whether Darren Wilson is indicted or not, the entire system is guilty, part III. In Kaba, M. (Ed.), *We Do This 'Til We Free Us: Abolitionist Organizing and Transforming Justice* (pp. 54–55). Haymarket Books: Chicago, IL.

Kraska, P. (2007). Militarization and policing: Its relevance to 21st century police. *Policing*, pp. 1–13. https://doi.org/10.1093/police/pam065.

López, A. R. (2019). "We know what the pigs don't like": The formation and solidarity of the original Rainbow Coalition. *Journal of African American Studies, 23*(4), 476–518. Retrieved from http://www.jstor.org/stable/45281880.

Ludwig, M. (2022). Biden is still issuing calls to increase police funding. *Truthout*. Retrieved from https://truthout.org/articles/biden-is-still-issuing-calls-to-increase-police-funding/.

Madeson, F. (2024). Michael Brown Jr.'s father is still fighting for justice and his son's legacy. *Truthout News*. Retrieved from https://truthout.org/articles/michael-brown-jr-s-father-is-still-fighting-for-justice-and-his-sons-legacy/.

Mapping Police Violence. (2024). *Data*. Reviewed and Retrieved on 2/12/24, from https://mappingpoliceviolence.org/?gclid=Cj0KCQiAq5meBhCyARIsAJrtdr50wA0FuRzvDKZ9_faC6z-SRch3Q0G9SckiAHu68Pg1FgMv4ceBxzMaAsBAEALw_wcB.

McKesson, D., Sinyangwe, S., Elzie, J., & Packnett, B. (2016). Police union contracts and police bill of rights analysis. *Campaign Zero*. Retrieved from https://campaignzero.org/wp-content/uploads/2022/11/CampaignZeroPoliceUnionContractReport-1.pdf.

Meko, H. (2024). N.Y.P.D. misconduct settlements cost $500 million over 6 years. *The New York Times*. Retrieved from https://www.nytimes.com/2024/02/29/nyregion/nypd-police-misconduct-settlements.html#:~:text=The%20board%20said%20it%20had,also%20take%20years%20to%20resolve.

Miller, L. (2015). Why cops kill: The psychology of police deadly force encounters. *Aggression and Behaviors, 22*, 97–111.

Mowatt, R. (2022). *The Geographies of Threat and the Production of Violence*. Routledge: New York, NY.

Muntaqim, J. (2020). *We Are Our Own Liberators*. Black Dragon Multimedia Management Enterprise: Rochester, NY.

NCJA (National Criminal Justice Association). (2024). A decade after Michael Brown shooting, reform record is mixed. *NCJA, Crime and Justice News*. Retrieved from https://www.ncja.org/crimeandjusticenews/a-decade-after-michael-brown-shooting-reform-record-is-mixed.

Obasogie, O. K., & Newman, Z. (2017). Police violence, use of force policies, and public health. *American Journal of Law & Medicine, 43*, 279–295.

Outland, R. (2021). Why black and brown youth fear and distrust police: An exploration of youth killed by police in the US (2016/2017), implications for counselors and service providers. *Open Journal of Social Science, 9*, 222–240. Retrieved from https://www.scirp.org/journal/paperinformation?paperid=108618.

Outland, R., Noel, T., Rounsville, K., Boatwright, T., Waleed, C., & Abraham, A. (2020). Living with trauma: Impact of police killings on the lives of the family and community of child and teen victims. *Current Psychology, 41*, 7059–7073. Retrieved from https://rdcu.be/cbkti.

Perry, I. (2021). Stop hustling black death Samaria Rice is the mother of Tamir, not a mother of the movement. *The Cut*. Retrieved from https://www.thecut.com/article/samaria-rice-profile.html.

Preston, C., & Bordon, J. (n.d.). Timeline: Laquan McDonald and attempts at police reform. *City Bureau*. Retrieved from https://www.citybureau.org/black-caucus-timeline.

Puente, M. (2019). LAPD ends another data-driven crime program touted to target violent offenders. *Los Angeles Times*. Retrieved from https://www.latimes.com/local/lanow/la-me-laser-lapd-crime-data-program-20190412-story.html.

Rodney, W. (1982). *How Europe Underdeveloped Africa*. Howard University Press: Washington, DC.

Rodney, W. (1996). *The Groundings with My Brothers*. School Times Publications: Chicago, IL.

Rodriguez, D. (2021). Tyranny of the task force: Police abolition and the counter-insurgent campus. *Connecticut Law Review, 506*. Retrieved from https://opencommons.uconn.edu/law_review/506.

Rodriguez, D. (2023). Chapter 12: The obsolescence of 'police brutality': Counterinsurgency in a moment of police reform. In Cunneen, C., Deckert, A., Porter, A., Tauri, J., & Webb, R. (Eds.), *The Routledge International Handbook on Decolonizing Justice*. Routledge: New York, NY.

Schuttler, J. F. (1991). The American Indian movement as a revolutionary organization. *Student Thesis, Dissertations, & Professional Papers No. 9337*. Retrieved from https://scholarworks.umt.edu/etd/9337.

Schweikert, J. R. (2020). Qualified immunity: A legal, practical, and moral failure. *Cato Institute, Policy Analysis No. 901*. Retrieved from https://papers.ssrn.com/sol3/papers.cfm?abstract_id=3694725.

Seigal, M. (2018a). Violence works: Policing and power. *Race & Class: Institute of Race Relations, 59*(4), 15–33.

Seigal, M. (2018b). *Violence Works: State Power and the Limits of Police*. Duke University Press Books: Durham, NC.

Shackford, S. (2020). Daniel Prude's brother called 911 because he was behaving erratically. Prude ended up dead. *Reason News*. Retrieved from https://reason.com/2020/09/03/daniel-prudes-brother-called-911-because-he-was-behaving-erratically-prude-ended-up-dead/?ocid=uxbndlbing.

Shoatz, R. M. (2013). *Maroon the Implacable: The Collected Writing of Russell Maroon Shoatz*. PM Press: Oakland, CA.

Staggers-Hakim, R. (2016). The nation's unprotected children and the ghost of Mike Brown, or the impact of national police killings on the health and social development of African American boys. *Journal of Human Behavior in the Social Environment, 26*(3–4), 390–399.

Sykes, W. G., & Taukolo, K. W. (2024). 'Mourning into a movement': Family members of George Floyd, Eric Garner discuss grief and activism at IOP forum. *The Harvard Crimson*. Retrieved from https://www.thecrimson.com/article/2024/4/19/iop-forum-grief-garner-floyd/.

Umoja, A. O. (2013). *We Will Shoot Back: Armed Resistance in the Mississippi Freedom Movement*. New York University Press: New York, NY.

Vargas, A. (2023). *Reporting on the Long Shadow of the LAPD's Data-Driven Policing Programs*. Health Equity & Social Justice, Center for Health Journalism: USC Annenberg. Retrieved from https://centerforhealthjournalism.org/our-work/insights/reporting-long-shadow-lapds-data-driven-policing-programs.

Vitale, A. S. (2018). *The End of Policing*. Verso: New York, NY.

Walker, S. (2001). *Police Accountability*. Wadsworth Thompson Learning: Belmont, CA.

Washington Post. (2024). *Police-Shootings-Database, 2015–2024.* Retrieved from https://www.washingtonpost.com/graphics/investigations/police-shootings-database/.

Wimbley, L. (2024). Michael Brown's mother seeks justice at international human rights hearing. *St. Louis Public Radio.* Retrieved from https://www.kcur.org/news/2024-07-11/michael-browns-mother-seeks-justice-at-international-human-rights-hearing.

Wittstock, L., & Salinas, E. J. (n.d.). A brief history of the American Indian movement. *American Indian Movement Grand Governing Council.* Retrieved from https://www.aimovement.org/ggc/history.html.

Zinn, H. (2003). *A People's History of the United States.* New Press: New York, NY.

6

IF NOT US THEN WHO?

Implications for Our Collective Involvement (Epilogue) Police Killings, Social Terror, and Cognitive Conditioning

As many readers can imagine and would agree, there appears to be a common link between police killings in the United States and what can be termed "social terror." Social terror can be understood as an individual's conscious and subconscious emotional, mental, and at times physical, responses to unchecked or continued institutionalized violence, terror, and death. A few examples of these forms of unchecked terror can include, but not limited to, police killings of poor people, international military warfare, and in some extreme cases, turf wars and intercommunal gang violence. For the sake of our work, we will focus attention on understanding the connection between police terrorism and social terror of the U.S. populace.

What initially led us to this line of inquiry was based on individuals' emotional, physical, and verbal responses to us researchers during fieldwork in 2018 and 2019. Specifically, while traveling through local communities in or near Rome and Brooklyn, NY, Newark and Toms River, NJ, Baltimore, MD, Los Angeles, CA, or Chicago, IL, we recall vividly on several occasions people either refusing to talk or did not want the talk to be recorded surrounding the death of a kid by police. For example, when approaching some people with the inquiry about our work, they walked in the opposite direction, waved us away while stating "I don't want to talk about that," whereas others openly expressed the topic as being "too traumatic to discuss." Some individuals expressed strong emotions when approached, such as crying, anger, and frustration, while others appeared skeptical, perceptively observant of who we were, and in turn, reminded us of the "safety precaution" for outsiders of the neighborhood (This encounter vividly occurred in LA

DOI: 10.4324/9781003665915-6

as well as Baltimore). A final example where individuals willing to talk to us, but refused to be audio or video recorded, thus making it difficult for us to capture the essence of these narratives.

After intense discourse and sense-making among the authors, we are convinced, and perhaps some readers of this work as well, that the phenomenon of police killings of U.S. residents has fueled and maintained a level of social terror in the mental and emotional states of many people. The underpinnings, or non-expressions related to these states, are reflective of what "can and cannot" be spoken about this phenomenon, especially in a public sphere that may be viewed by a mass audience. Some may describe this type of stagnant, immobile expression of truth as "cognitive conditioning." Cognitive conditioning can be described as the continued exposure to external stimuli (police killings) that leads to a refusal to create and form new thought patterns, thinking, ways of knowing or understanding. Thus, there currently exists the possibility that police's ability to kill 1,000+ U.S. residents each year, with impunity, alongside media propaganda of police as "good cops," results in high levels of individual fear and apprehension to discuss, analyze, and in turn, make sense of U.S. police terrorism of urban and rural communities. Plain and simply put: People are afraid.

In conclusion, many will read this section, utter under their breath or in their thoughts, "yeah this might be true," while continuing on with their daily lives. Work, shopping, caregiving, socializing, etc. continue on with their daily lives. Some people may believe that staying silent, complacent, or simply ignoring the phenomenon of police killings in the United States is a form of social safety or social acceptance by those who maintain the status quo. However, as a society, we create a dangerous social predicament for ourselves, elders, women, and children when we attempt to *mask* social terror with social safety. If we are true to ourselves and others, it is impossible for the two phenomena to exist simultaneously. Thus, in order to truly foster and harbor a society that is socially safe for all members of the public, it becomes necessary to eliminate any and all forms of social terror from our reality, including police terrorism. Please consider . . .

On a final note, while we intend for this work to be shared with a broad audience of readers from diverse disciplines, professions, and the general public, we also offer specific implications and recommendations for educators, counselors and service providers, youth, and finally, activists. These implications are not meant to encourage siloed organizing and strategizing to address this phenomenon. But they are meant to do the opposite: To help readers observe how our collective and united efforts can act as efficient means to combat youth killed by police in the United States and beyond.

Implications for Educators and Service Providers

First, our peers, or educators, must do our best to share relevant historical and contemporary information to assist students in deepening their understanding of this phenomenon. Specifically, educators can utilize this book, along with useful references and resources (Abu-Jamal, 2016; Hill, 2010; Kraska, 2007; Seigal, 2018; Umoja, 2013; Vitale, 2018), to facilitate class lectures, campus presentations, and community forums about youth killed by police and the impact on survivors. This can be achieved by including this work and similar ones as required readings in curricula for high schoolers, undergraduate, and graduate students. In doing so, educators can work with their collegiate peers and students to create innovative strategies and programs to 1) uplift the narratives of survivors (Outland et al., 2020; Staggers-Hakim, 2016) and 2) implement and experiment with solutions to dissolve elements that maintain police killings with impunity in the United States (i.e., Police Unions, LEOBORs, and Qualified Immunity – Bies, 2017; Fegley, 2020; Fisk & Richardson, 2017; Halvorson, 2022; McKesson et al., 2016).

In addition, educators can lead critical research studies (hopefully qualitative) with students and interdisciplinary peers to capture the narrative of survivors impacted by youth killed by police. For example, educators can invite students and interdisciplinary scholars to utilize the Methodology and Findings from this project and phase I (Living with Trauma scholarship; Outland et al., 2020) to partake in a state or national research study. At the moment, states including Texas, Northern California, Nevada, Arizona, and Missouri are examples of those with a high prevalence of citizenry killed by police, which these states have yet to be explored by the researchers (Mapping Police Violence, 2024). Thus, we invite and encourage educators to join the intellectual struggle to develop and implement ideas that can put a halt to youth killed by police in the United States, with impunity. Our unified efforts as educators can create a new wave of student scholars committed to using their knowledge, skills, and abilities to challenge state-sanctioned violence by police, while providing an alternative narrative of what happened to youth victims: Survivors' Narratives.

Counselors and service providers (social workers, nurses, doctors, lawyers, etc.) have an important role to fulfill regarding potential healing, restitution, and reparation experienced by survivors and loved ones of youth victims. Specifically, according to our travels during this project, it was very problematic to learn from survivors and community members impacted by a youth killed by police that the research team was the *first and only* individuals to check in on them. As humanity, we can do better. Doing better can entail counselors and social workers collectivizing their intention, will, and efforts

FIGURE 6.1 Overlook from a hillside at a park in Capital Heights, MD.

to *visit* the community of survivors, or where the police killing occurred, while talking and being with local residents. It is relevant for these service professionals to explore the needs, challenges, and desires of survivors in the aftermath of experiencing a violent and traumatic death (Baddeley et al., 2015; Bogensperger & Lueger-Schuster, 2014; Denderen et al., 2017). Why is this important? Research suggest that individuals who experience violent or traumatic death are likely to encounter short- and long-term complex grief (Denderen et al., 2017; Nakajima et al., 2012), which can include depression and anxiety (Djelantik et al., 2017), ruminating thoughts about the occurrence (Heeke et al., 2017), issues with sleeping, as well as suicidal ideations (Kaltman & Bonanno, 2001). Thus, exploring the mental, emotional, and material needs of survivors, while applying trauma-informed interventions (Huang, 2018; Lichtenthal et al., 2010; Rheingold et al., 2015; Rheingold & Williams, 2018; Saindon et al., 2014; Smid et al., 2015; Stiles, 2020), can be a useful strategy to assist victims in finding healing in the aftermath of these occurrences.

Yet, we are still faced with a major dilemma: Survivors' experiences of healing without justice. Healing without justice is a fact of the matter that police kill youth with impunity, or are rarely if ever held accountable. Thus, as discussed in a previous chapter, a restitution and reparation process is necessary to uphold the principle and practice of justice and accountability (Bukhari, 2010; Kaba, 2021; Rodney, 1996; Shakur, 2011). Counselors and service providers, along with trusted elders, critical lawyers, and activists, can play a vital role in facilitating a restitution and reparation process. Since details of this process were previously discussed, we will refrain from repeating them here. Yet, what must be understood as a potential outcome of this process, is that 1) this process can be understood as originating from the experiences of survivors or loved ones impacted by a youth killed by police; the 2) outcomes can be embraced, implemented, and upheld by local service officials, with the support of community members who believe in and practice justice; and most importantly, 3) this process occurs external to the U.S. colonial judicial system that continues to permit police to take the life of children with impunity. Thus, we extend a sincere call to counselors and service providers to identify survivors and community members impacted by youth killed by police and make it our mission to act as conduits of healing, justice, and accountability for these individuals.

Implications for Youth

The implications for youth impacted by this phenomenon are highly important. Specifically, many youth experience the mental, emotional, and social devastations related to youth killed by police (Rheingold et al., 2015; Staggers-Hakim, 2016). Alongside the suffering of simply learning of a peer killed in a violent way by someone who was supposed to protect them, youth also have to grapple with the media propaganda of criminalizing their deceased friend, and in turn, *Justifying why* the police killed the child (Outland et al., 2020). Youth are left in a conundrum of learning of a peer killed in a violent way by police, while in turn, also learning that nothing will be done about it. As a result, what message is relayed to our children? It appears that the message is one that our kids are disposable, unimportant, and only criminals when killed at the behest of police (Hill, 2017). Thus, this message and phenomenon must be transformed. K-12 educators, along with parents and youth advocates, must inform youth of the "Truth" regarding the purpose and practices of policing (Seigal, 2018). Such truth can be found in Chapters 2 and 4 of this work. The resources and references included in this project can also be used for educating youth on policing. Finally, adults must be courageous enough to 1) have conversations with youth about other youth killed by police, 2) explore youth understanding of the phenomenon, and in turn, 3) assist youth to organize their efforts and will to address the issue. In other words, whether these processes transpire at youth's school, home, or community, important outcomes that can follow include 1) helping youth heal following violent and traumatic death of a friend, peer, or classmate and 2) trusted adults supporting youth to raise their voices, energy, and will as organizing tools to challenge state-sanctioned violence by police (Kaba, 2021). If adults do not assist our youth with these processes to address youth killed by police, then eventually our youth will take matters into their own hands and determine the appropriate remedy to the circumstances by any oppressed people (Fanon, 2004).

Implications for Activists

On a final note, we extend implications to the courageous activists and organizers against youth killed by police. Activists and organizers sacrifice a lot of their being, livelihood, and at times, family, in order to struggle against police terrorism of poor communities (Abu-Jamal, 2016; Bukhari, 2010; Muntaqim, 2020; Schuttler, 1991; Umoja, 2013; Whitaker, 2023). Findings from this project identify concrete experiences regarding the suffering and hardships of activists and organizers. Thus, these individuals are also traumatized, and in turn, continue to fight for justice in the aftermath of youth killed by police. Thus, while activists and organizers play their role to transform and dissipate policing in the United States as we know it, they also need hands-on support from the local community. Such support can include material resources (i.e., food, clothing, shelter, money, gainful employment, etc.), mental and emotional services, along with political alignment with local politicians and council members (i.e., developing law and policy that reflect the demands of local organizers). Critical lawyers can also be vital resources and support for activists and organizers. For example, they have legal power and knowledge to educate organizers of their rights if apprehended or terrorized by police while organizing. They can also act as activists' standing attorneys in cases when they are brought to court due to organizing efforts; in turn, attorneys can legally challenge any court charges against activists (Franklin et al., 2025). As we learned from this project, survivors and family members are transformed into activists in the aftermath of their youthful loved one killed by police. If we know this to be true and survivors experience complex grief following a violent or traumatic death, then it is likely that activists and organizers can benefit from ongoing support, check-ins, inquiries, as well as healing practices, extended by counselors and service providers.

Similarly, educators can play a vital role to protect *student activists* from administrative and institutional repression due to their activism on campus and in the community. In recent times, student activists in higher education have experienced physical, academic, and psycho-social repression from internal and external forces due to their organizing efforts to end the Israeli occupation and genocide against the Palestinian people (Alvarez, 2025; Higgins, 2024; Nashed, 2024; Palestine Legal, 2024). Student activists' repression by administration and campus police has included physical assaults and violent disruption of student encampments, school suspension and expulsion, withholding students' diplomas and degrees, criminal charges, and FBI raids of student residence halls and local family residences. In this regard, college campuses and K-12 schools are criminalizing students' and faculties' organizing and activism efforts, which in turn, sets an unintended precedence against student activists that portrays a conclusion that *those who organize on and off campus will be censored and punished*.

Thus, educators can play a vital role to disrupt this systemic repression in several ways. First, we can explore, understand, and speak up about the ways college and K-12 administration and others target, repress, and punish student and faculty activists. In doing this, second, we can organize with trusted members of the academic and local community to conjure and implement strategies to actively protect and speak up on behalf of student organizers (Biondi, 2012). Educators and student leaders must find ways to persuade and move campus and school administration to work with and support activists on and off campus, and not against them. Indeed, this posture is a courageous one taken by any college administrator or K-12 principal, primarily due to the external economic and political pressures to adhere to status quo sanctions against educators and student activists (Gowayed, 2024; Haidar & Kettles, 2024; Speri, 2025; Taft, 2024). Thus, educators and trusted allies must find creative ways to build and organize a campus or school culture and climate that celebrate and uplift student activism due to their necessity in a society predicated on state-sanctioned and deputized violence. In doing this, educators and student activists, along with members of the campus community who believe in justice and freedom for all, will no longer have to exist in a state of fear, self-silencing, and moral decay that typifies the current state of all out repression, violence, and trauma by campus administration against activists of the college community.

In conclusion, a collective and unified effort is needed. As educators, service providers, youth, and activists, we must put aside our differences, attempt to listen and sit with one another, while partaking in extensive learning, discourse, and practices (i.e., praxis) to address police killings in the U.S. history shows that we cannot rely on the judicial system or the government to end this phenomenon: Police violence domestically in the United States is an extension of a larger apparatus of state-sanctioned and deputized violence and militancy, globally (Abu-Jamal & Vittoria, 2018; Burton, 2023; Hess, 2000; Khalidi, 2013). Thus, all efforts, will, intent, and energy are welcomed from ALL who wish to see this phenomenon come to an end. Otherwise, as we now understand with youth killed by police with impunity, we all will remain disposable colonial subjects.

References

Abu-Jamal, M. (2016). *We Want Freedom: A Life in the Black Panther Party.* Common Notions: Brooklyn, NY.

Abu-Jamal, M., & Vittoria, S. (2018). *Murder Incorporated: Empire, Genocide, & Manifest Destiny.* Prison Radio Prison Radio: San Francisco, CA.

Alvarez, M. (2025). *The Student Movement Turns to Hunger Striking to Call for Justice in Palestine.* Retrieved from https://inthesetimes.com/article/student-movement-turns-hunger-strike-for-palestine.

Baddeley, J. L., Williams, J. L., Rynearson, T., Correa, F., Saindon, C., & Rheingold, A. A. (2015). Death thoughts and images in treatment-seekers after violent loss. *Death Studies, 39*, 84–91. https://doi.org/10.1080/07481187.2014.893274.

Bies, K. J. (2017). Let the sunshine in: Illuminating the powerful role police unions play in shielding officer misconduct. *Stanford Law & Policy Review, 28*(1), 109-[vi].

Biondi, M. (2012). *The Black revolution on campus.* Univ of California Press.: Los Angeles, CA.

Bogensperger, J., & Lueger-Schuster, B. (2014). Losing a child: Finding meaning in bereavement. *European Journal of Psychotraumatology, 5*(1), 1–9. https://doi.org/10.3402/ejpt.v5.22910.

Bukhari, S. (2010). *The War Before: The True Life Story of Becoming a Black Panther, Keeping the Faith in Prison & Fighting for Those Left Behind.* The Feminist Press: New York, NY.

Burton, O. (2023). *Tip of the Spear: Black Radicalism, Prison Repression, and the Long Attica Revolt.* University of California Press: Oakland, CA.

Denderen, M. V., Keijser, J. D., Stewart, R., & Boelen, P. A. (2017). Treating complicated grief and posttraumatic stress in homicidally bereaved individuals: A randomized controlled trial. *Clinical Psychology and Psychotherapy, 25*(4), 497–508.

Djelantik, M. J., Smid, G. E., Kleber, R. J., & Boelen, P. A. (2017). Symptoms of prolonged grief, post-traumatic stress, and depression after loss in a Dutch community sample: A latent class analysis. *Psychiatry Research, 247*, 276–281. http://dx.doi.org/10.1016/j.psychres.2016.11.023.

Fanon, F. (2004). *The Wretched of the Earth.* Grove Press: New York, NY.

Fegley, T. (2020). Police unions and officer privileges. *The Independent Review, 25*(2), 165–186.

Fisk, C. L., & Richardson, L. (2017). Police unions. *George Washington Law Review, 85*(3), 712–799.

Franklin, K., Parker, M., & Herskind, M. (2025). *No Cop City, No Cop World.* Haymarket Books: Chicago, IL.

Gowayed, H. (2024). *Pro-Palestine Campus Encampments and Israel's Targeting of American Students.* Arab Center: Washington DC. Retrieved from https://arabcenterdc.org/resource/pro-palestine-campus-encampments-and-israels-targeting-of-american-students/.

Haidar, E. H., & Kettles, C. E. (2024). Outrage at decision to deny diplomas to 13 pro-Palestine students overshadows Harvard commencement. *The Harvard Crimson.* Retrieved from https://www.thecrimson.com/article/2024/5/24/commencement-overshadowed-proPalestine-outrage/#:~:text=Advertisement-,Outrage%20at%20Decision%20to%20Deny%20Diplomas%20to%2013%20Pro%2DPalestine,The%20faculty%20had%20spoken.%E2%80%9D.

Halvorson, J. T. (2022). *The Impact of Police Unions on the Prosecution of Officers, Legitimacy, and Reform.* Southern Illinois University Carbondale, OpenSIUC: Carbondale. Retrieved from https://opensiuc.lib.siu.edu/gs_rp.

Heeke, C., Kampisiou, C., Niemeyer, H., & Knaevelsrud, C. (2017). A systematic review and meta-analysis of correlates of prolonged grief disorder in adults exposed to violent loss. *European Journal of Psychotraumatology, 8*(6), 1583524. https://doi.org/10.1080/20008198.2019.1583524.

Hess, P. (2000). *Overturning the Culture of Violence.* Burning Spear Publication: St. Petersburg, FL.

Higgins, V. (2024). Haldane discusses the role of law in the struggle for Palestinian liberation. *Socialist Lawyer, 95*, 14–15.

Hill, G. (2010). *500 Years of Indigenous Resistance.* PM Press: Oakland, CA.

Hill, M. L. (2017). *Nobody: Casualties of America's War on the Vulnerable, from Ferguson to Flint and Beyond.* Atria Paperback: New York, NY.

Huang, L. (2018). *Unmet Needs and Service Satisfaction of Victim Support for the Direct and Indirect Victims of Serious Violence: Results from a Cross-Sectional Survey in Taiwan.* https://doi.org/10.1371/journal.

Kaba, M. (2021). *We Do This 'Til We Free Us: Abolitionist Organizing and Transforming Justice.* Haymarket Books: Chicago, IL.

Kaltman, S., & Bonanno, G. A. (2001). Trauma and bereavement: Examining the impact of sudden and violent deaths. *Anxiety Disorders, 17*, 131–147.

Khalidi, R. (2013). *Brokers of Deceit: How the U.S. Has Undermined Peace in the Middle East.* Beacon Press: Boston, MA.

Kraska, P. (2007). Militarization and policing: Its relevance to 21st century police. *Policing,* pp. 1–13. https://doi.org/10.1093/police/pam065.

Lichtenthal, W. G., Joseph, M. C., Robert, A. N., & Keesee, N. J. (2010). Sense and significance: A mixed methods examination of meaning making after the loss of one's child. *Journal of Clinical Psychology, 66*(7), 791–812.

Mapping Police Violence. (2024). *Data.* Reviewed and Retrieved on 2/12/24, from https://mappingpoliceviolence.org/?gclid=Cj0KCQiAq5meBhCyARIsAJrtdr50wA0FuRzvDKZ9_faC6z-SRch3Q0G9SckiAHu68Pg1FgMv4ceBxzMaAsBAEALw_wcB.

McKesson, D., Sinyangwe, S., Elzie, J., & Packnett, B. (2016). Police union contracts and police bill of rights analysis. *Campaign Zero.* Retrieved from https://campaignzero.org/wp-content/uploads/2022/11/CampaignZeroPoliceUnionContractReport-1.pdf.

Muntaqim, J. (2020). *We Are Our Own Liberators*. Black Dragon Multimedia Management Enterprise: Rochester, NY.

Nakajima, S., Masaya, I., Akemi, S., Takako, K., & Konishi, T. (2012). Complicated grief in those bereaved by violent death: The effects of post-traumatic stress disorder on complicated grief. *Dialogues in Clinical Neuroscience*, *14*(2), 210–214.

Nashed, M. (2024). *US campus protests of Israeli 'genocide' offer hope to students from Gaza*. Retrieved from https://www.aljazeera.com/features/2024/5/6/us-student-protests-of-israeli-genocide-offer-hope-to-students-from-gaza.

Outland, R., Noel, T., Rounsville, K., Boatwright, T., Waleed, C., & Abraham, A. (2020). Living with trauma: Impact of police killings on the lives of the family and community of child and teen victims. *Current Psychology*, *41*, 7059–7073. Retrieved from https://rdcu.be/cbkti.

Palestine Legal. (2024). *Statement by two Palestinian students who have faced severe university retaliation for protesting Israel's Genocide in Gaza*. Retrieved from https://palestinelegal.org/news/2024/10/16/statement-by-two-palestinian-students-who-have-faced-severe-university-retaliation-for-protesting-israels-genocide-in-gaza.

Quinn, R. (2024). DePaul adjunct ousted for optional Gaza assignment. *Inside Higher Ed*. Retrieved from https://www.insidehighered.com/news/faculty-issues/academic-freedom/2024/06/03/depaul-adjunct-ousted-optional-gaza-assignment.

Rheingold, A. A., Baddeley, J. L., Williams, J. L., Brown, C., Wallace, M. M., Correa, F., & Rynearson, E. K. (2015). Restorative retelling for violent death: An investigation of treatment effectiveness, influencing factors, and durability. *Journal of Loss and Trauma*, *20*, 541–555.

Rheingold, A. A., & Williams, J. L. (2018). Module-based comprehensive approach for addressing heterogeneous mental health sequelae of violent loss survivors. *Death Studies*, *42*(3), 164–171. https://doi.org/10.1080/07481187.2017.1370798.

Rodney, W. (1996). *The Groundings with My Brothers*. School Times Publications: Chicago, IL.

Saindon, C., Rheingold, A. A., Baddeley, J., Wallace, M. M., Brown, C., & Rynearson, E. K. (2014). Restorative retelling for violent loss: An open clinical trial. *Death Studies*, *38*, 251–258. https://doi.org/10.1080/07481187.2013.783654.

Schuttler, J. F. (1991). The American Indian movement as a revolutionary organization. *Student Thesis, Dissertations, & Professional Papers No. 9337*. Retrieved from https://scholarworks.umt.edu/etd/9337.

Seigal, M. (2018). Violence works: Policing and power. *Race & Class: Institute of Race Relations*, *59*(4), 15–33.

Shakur, M. (2011, January 1). *Justice and Amnesty: Applying the South African Truth and Reconciliation Process to the North American Black Liberation Movement*. Truth and Reconciliation Commission in the United States. Retrieved from https://mutulushakur.com/wp-content/uploads/2014/03/TRC-booklet.pdf.

Smid, G. E., Kleber, R. J., de la Rie, S. M., Bos, J. B. A., Gersons, B. P. R., & Boelen, P. A. (2015). Brief eclectic psychotherapy for traumatic grief (BEP-TG): Toward integrated treatment of symptoms related to traumatic loss. *European Journal of Psychotraumatology*, *6*(1), 27324. https://doi.org/10.3402/ejpt.v6.27324.

Speri, A. (2025). Punishing pro-Palestine protests. *Aljazeera*. Retrieved from https://www.aljazeera.com/news/longform/2025/2/19/us-universities-target-pro-palestine-students-with-suspensions-campus-bans.

Staggers-Hakim, R. (2016). The nation's unprotected children and the ghost of Mike Brown, or the impact of national police killings on the health and social development of African American boys. *Journal of Human Behavior in the Social Environment*, *26*(3–4), 390–399.

Stiles, K. (2020). The long term effect of bereavement and grief with a highly-publicized violent death. *Journal of Loss and Trauma*. https://doi.org/10.1080/15325024.2020.1727670.

Taft, I. (2024). How universities cracked down on pro-Palestinian activism. *The New York Times*. Retrieved from https://www.nytimes.com/2024/11/25/us/university-crackdowns-protests-israel-hamas-war.html.

Umoja, A. O. (2013). *We Will Shoot Back: Armed Resistance in the Mississippi Freedom Movement*. New York University Press: New York, NY.

Vitale, A. S. (2018). *The End of Policing*. Verso: New York, NY.

Whitaker, M. (2023). *Saying It Loud: 1966 – The Year Black Power Challenged the Civil Rights Movement*. Simon & Schuster: New York, NY.

INDEX